T0209458

MACAT

An Analysis of

James Surowiecki's

The Wisdom of Crowds:
Why the Many are Smarter than the Few and How Collective Wisdom Shapes Business, Economics, Societies, and Nations

Nikki Springer

ROUTLEDGE

Published by Macat International Ltd
24:13 Coda Centre, 189 Munster Road, London SW6 6AW.

Distributed exclusively by Routledge
2 Park Square, Milton Park, Abingdon, Oxon OX14 4RN
711 Third Avenue, New York, NY 10017, USA

Routledge is an imprint of the Taylor & Francis Group, an informa business

www.macat.com
info@macat.com

Cataloguing in Publication Data
A catalogue record for this book is available from the British Library.
Library of Congress Cataloguing-in-Publication Data is available upon request.
Cover illustration: David Newton

ISBN 978-1-912453-48-1 (hardback)
ISBN 978-1-912453-03-0 (paperback)
ISBN 978-1-912453-18-4 (e-book)

Notice
The information in this book is designed to orientate readers of the work under analysis,
to elucidate and contextualise its key ideas and themes, and to aid in the development
of critical thinking skills. It is not meant to be used, nor should it be used, as a
substitute for original thinking or in place of original writing or research. References and
notes are provided for informational purposes and their presence does not constitute
endorsement of the information or opinions therein. This book is presented solely for
educational purposes. It is sold on the understanding that the publisher is not engaged
to provide any scholarly advice. The publisher has made every effort to ensure that
this book is accurate and up-to-date, but makes no warranties or representations with
regard to the completeness or reliability of the information it contains. The information
and the opinions provided herein are not guaranteed or warranted to produce particular
results and may not be suitable for students of every ability. The publisher shall not be
liable for any loss, damage or disruption arising from any errors or omissions, or from
the use of this book, including, but not limited to, special, incidental, consequential or
other damages caused, or alleged to have been caused, directly or indirectly, by the
information contained within.

CONTENTS

THE MACAT LIBRARY

The Macat Library is a series of unique academic explorations of seminal works in the humanities and social sciences – books and papers that have had a significant and widely recognised impact on their disciplines. It has been created to serve as much more than just a summary of what lies between the covers of a great book. It illuminates and explores the influences on, ideas of, and impact of that book. Our goal is to offer a learning resource that encourages critical thinking and fosters a better, deeper understanding of important ideas.

Each publication is divided into three Sections: Influences, Ideas, and Impact. Each Section has four Modules. These explore every important facet of the work, and the responses to it.

This Section-Module structure makes a Macat Library book easy to use, but it has another important feature. Because each Macat book is written to the same format, it is possible (and encouraged!) to cross-reference multiple Macat books along the same lines of inquiry or research. This allows the reader to open up interesting interdisciplinary pathways.

To further aid your reading, lists of glossary terms and people mentioned are included at the end of this book (these are indicated by an asterisk [*] throughout) – as well as a list of works cited.

Macat has worked with the University of Cambridge to identify the elements of critical thinking and understand the ways in which six different skills combine to enable effective thinking.
Three allow us to fully understand a problem; three more give us the tools to solve it. Together, these six skills make up the **PACIER** model of critical thinking. They are:

ANALYSIS – understanding how an argument is built
EVALUATION – exploring the strengths and weaknesses of an argument
INTERPRETATION – understanding issues of meaning

CREATIVE THINKING – coming up with new ideas and fresh connections
PROBLEM-SOLVING – producing strong solutions
REASONING – creating strong arguments

To find out more, visit **WWW.MACAT.COM.**

CRITICAL THINKING AND *THE WISDOM OF CROWDS*

Primary critical thinking skill: PROBLEM SOLVING
Secondary critical thinking skill: REASONING

The Wisdom of Crowds solves a problem that had baffled academics for generations: how can a crowd, the members of which are not individually distinguished, arrive at solutions that elude individual experts?

Surowiecki shows why the group is often smarter than the individual and that the aggregation of information from non-experts can often be more accurate than individual expert opinion. To demonstrate this, he presents anecdotes drawn from society and nature that all utilize the principles of crowd intelligence and the aggregation of information to reach near-perfect conclusions.

Surowiecki classifies crowd intelligence into three main categories: cognition, coordination, and cooperation, and his book provides a clearly defined structure that allows organizations to tap the wealth of knowledge contained within their own teams, as well as providing guidance for ensuring that knowledge is useful. *The Wisdom of Crowds* is classified as a business, management, and psychology book, and addresses the three fields equally well.

The author outlines three major criteria for ensuring that the insight and conclusions of crowds is as accurate as possible; individuals within a wise crowd must be decentralized, possess cognitive diversity, and be independent. But what makes *The Wisdom of Crowds* so successful is Surowiecki's ability to engage a variety of readers, from everyday members of the public to subject matter experts and corporate executives. He weaves together current and historical anecdotes with overarching principles that are applicable to numerous other examples. Trained as a financial journalist, Surowiecki's work is fluid, witty, and memorable, ensuring that the lessons learned from his work are easily retained for future application.

ABOUT THE AUTHOR OF THE ORIGINAL WORK

James Surowiecki is an American journalist born in Meriden, Connecticut, in 1967. After graduating with a PhD in American Studies from Yale University, he established himself as a prominent financial journalist. He was a regular finance contributor at *The New Yorker*, a popular American magazine. Surowiecki had a knack for combining economic theory with practical, real-world application and captivating readers with fluid, energetic prose. He published *The Wisdom of Crowds: Why the Many Are Smarter Than the Few and How Collective Wisdom Shapes Business, Economies, Societies and Nations*, in 2004. Surowiecki lives in Brooklyn, New York, and is married to journalist Meghan O'Rourke.

ABOUT THE AUTHOR OF THE ANALYSIS

Nikki Johnson Springer is currently a joint MBA and PhD Student at Yale University. Her dissertation focuses on the development of utility-scale solar energy on public lands in the American Southwest and the competing needs of industry incentives, habitat conservation, and federal regulation.

Springer is the former Garvan Chair & Visiting Professor in Landscape Architecture at the University of Arkansas and has worked in design and sustainability roles for Walmart and the Walt Disney Company. She holds a Master of Landscape Architecture and Master of Urban Planning from Harvard University and a Bachelor of Science in Architecture from the Massachusetts Institute of Technology.

ABOUT MACAT

GREAT WORKS FOR CRITICAL THINKING

Macat is focused on making the ideas of the world's great thinkers accessible and comprehensible to everybody, everywhere, in ways that promote the development of enhanced critical thinking skills.

It works with leading academics from the world's top universities to produce new analyses that focus on the ideas and the impact of the most influential works ever written across a wide variety of academic disciplines. Each of the works that sit at the heart of its growing library is an enduring example of great thinking. But by setting them in context – and looking at the influences that shaped their authors, as well as the responses they provoked – Macat encourages readers to look at these classics and game-changers with fresh eyes. Readers learn to think, engage and challenge their ideas, rather than simply accepting them.

'Macat offers an amazing first-of-its-kind tool for interdisciplinary learning and research. Its focus on works that transformed their disciplines and its rigorous approach, drawing on the world's leading experts and educational institutions, opens up a world-class education to anyone.'

Andreas Schleicher
Director for Education and Skills, Organisation for Economic
Co-operation and Development

'Macat is taking on some of the major challenges in university education … They have drawn together a strong team of active academics who are producing teaching materials that are novel in the breadth of their approach.'

Prof Lord Broers,
former Vice-Chancellor of the University of Cambridge

'The Macat vision is exceptionally exciting. It focuses upon new modes of learning which analyse and explain seminal texts which have profoundly influenced world thinking and so social and economic development. It promotes the kind of critical thinking which is essential for any society and economy. This is the learning of the future.'

Rt Hon Charles Clarke, former UK Secretary of State for Education

'The Macat analyses provide immediate access to the critical conversation surrounding the books that have shaped their respective discipline, which will make them an invaluable resource to all of those, students and teachers, working in the field.'

Professor William Tronzo, University of California at San Diego

WAYS IN TO THE TEXT

KEY POINTS

- James Surowiecki is a popular American writer who writes on a variety of business, psychology, and economic topics.

- *The Wisdom of Crowds* highlights several current and historical examples of the knowledge power of crowds.

- The book makes the argument that, under the correct conditions, crowds can be more intelligent than experts.

Who Is James Surowiecki?

James Surowiecki was born in Meriden, Connecticut, in 1967. After spending time in Puerto Rico as a child, his family returned to Connecticut and he graduated from Choate Rosemary Hall, a competitive private boarding school, in 1984. Surowiecki was a Morehead scholar at the University of North Carolina at Chapel Hill, class of 1988, where he earned highest honors. He continued his academic work with a PhD in American Studies from Yale University as a Mellon Fellowship recipient. He currently lives in Brooklyn, New York, and is married to Meghan O'Rourke, a journalist and editor at *Slate* magazine.[1]

Surowiecki is a popular magazine and book writer and writes primarily on non-fiction topics in business, psychology, and economics. He began his journalism career at *The New York Times* in

2000, where he focused on business and finance. He later wrote for *Fortune, Slate, The New Yorker,* the *Wall Street Journal,* and the *Washington Post.* At *Slate,* he was the author of the "Moneybox" column. His articles span a wide range of topics, from college sports to finance and American culture.[2] In 2017, Surowiecki announced he was leaving *The New Yorker* after 17 years. He stated: "I'm going to be working on a book (or books) and looking for other interesting projects."[3]

What Does *The Wisdom of Crowds* Say?

Surowiecki writes in his book, *The Wisdom of Crowds,* published in 2004, that "The idea of the wisdom of crowds is not that a group will always give you the right answer but that on average it will consistently come up with a better answer than any individual could provide."[4] The idea of "crowd knowledge"* or the aggregation of knowledge from a large group of unrelated individuals, is not unique to Surowiecki; however, his treatment of the theory and its application is novel and compelling.

The Wisdom of Crowds describes and critiques the general knowledge and problem-solving capabilities contained in diverse crowds. The book is divided into four thematic sections. In the first section, Surowiecki gives a variety of examples of this idea in practice, from guessing the weight of an ox at a country fair to locating a missing submarine in the middle of the ocean and identifying the cause of a space shuttle explosion. He categorizes three types of decision-making scenarios that are best analyzed or solved with collective intelligence:* (1) cognition problems,* (2) coordination problems,* and (3) cooperation problems.*

The second section of the book identifies four main criteria necessary for crowds to offer meaningful intelligence and insight. These criteria are (1) diversity of opinion, (2) independence of individual opinion, (3) decentralization,* and (4) aggregation.* These criteria, although often overlooked, are critical to Surowiecki's entire argument, and form the basis for much of his defence against criticism.

The third section differentiates between intelligent crowds like the ones Surowiecki describes in beautifully articulated examples and instances where crowd behaviour becomes swayed incorrectly, hysterical, manic, or dangerous. The section provides insight into determining how to tell between a crowd that is wise one that would be savvy to take their cues from the crowd and one that is hysterical and mad, such as the dot-com investors.*

The fourth and final section gives recommendations for implementing crowd wisdom* for decision-making within one's organization, and how designing information-seeking initiatives, such as employee surveys, can be modified to best apply crowd wisdom practices. The argument of the book is that relying on the expert can be a mistake and can be a costly one. "…attempting to 'chase the expert,' looking for the one man who will have the answers to an organization's problem, is a waste of time."[5]

While the book draws on several historical examples and makes the case for tapping the crowd knowledge resource of an organization, probably the most relevant and promising application of Surowiecki's theory is through the immense crowd aggregation* opportunities available online, via such applications as prediction markets, stock market predictions, and crowdsourcing.* *The Wisdom of Crowds* was first published in 2004 and has been reprinted several times since.

Why Does *The Wisdom of Crowds* Matter?

The Wisdom of Crowds reminds us of the power of new ways of thinking, of asking questions already thought to have been answered, and of reconsidering a new approach. It reminds us of the power of the general population and the different ways one can source knowledge and opinions. From an organizational management perspective, it provides guidance and insight into ways in which organizational leaders can structure problem-solving efforts to take full advantage of the collective wisdom* already held within the organization. But it also provides guidance on the limitations of this resource. *The Wisdom of Crowds* can help us collectively avoid such things as the next economic bubble, the next mass hysteria, or the next mass adoption of obsolete infrastructure.

Surowiecki's work also lays the foundation for a number of group collaboration and innovation, much toward the same type of loose, flat organizations as the Linux/Unix developers Surowiecki describes. "There's a revolution brewing that is about to end the world of work as we know it. We are fast approaching a tipping point, where new capacities for mass collaboration will completely redefine the work we do and the way we work. Technological innovations now make it possible for large numbers of people to work together without going through a central organization and they can do it smarter, faster, and cheaper."[6]

NOTES

1 "Weddings: Meghan O'Rourke, James Surowiecki," *The New York Times*, July 22, 2007, accessed November 9, 2017, http://www.nytimes.com/2007/07/22/fashion/weddings/22orourke.html.

2 "James Surowiecki Contributor Biography," *The New Yorker*, accessed November 8, 2017, https://www.newyorker.com/contributors/james-surowiecki.

3 Roush, Chris, "Surowiecki leaves *The New Yorker*" *Talking Biz News*, March 11, 2017, accessed November 7, 2017, http://talkingbiznews.com/1/surowiecki-leaves-the-new-yorker.

4 James Surowiecki, *The Wisdom of Crowds* (New York: Anchor Books, 2004), 289.

5 James Surowiecki, *The Wisdom of Crowds*, C-SPAN. June 10, 2004, accessed November 10, 2017,   https://www.c-span.org/video/?182386-1/the-wisdom-crowds.

6 Rod Collins, "Review excerpt on book cover," *The Wisdom of Crowds,* (New York: Anchor Books, 2004), cover.

SECTION 1
INFLUENCES

MODULE 1
THE AUTHOR AND THE HISTORICAL CONTEXT

KEY POINTS

- *The Wisdom of Crowds* remains solid guidance for capturing the knowledge of large crowds and avoiding mania* in large groups.

- Surowiecki's tenure at *The New Yorker* helped groom his ability to merge economic and financial theory with current and historic events.

- The trend toward knowledge aggregation* on the internet prompted Surowiecki to explore the theories that govern crowd wisdom.

Why Read This Text?

James Surowiecki's *The Wisdom of Crowds* revisits a century-old theory of "crowd" or collective intelligence but sheds new light, and new enthusiasm, on the topic. Collective intelligence, sometimes called opinion aggregation,* is a core concept in politics, biology, economics, and risk assessment,* and is becoming more important in criminal forensics* investigations

The Wisdom of Crowds provides us with a unique perspective on the power of ourselves and the ways in which we can come together to accomplish huge tasks. Through the creative use of case study examples from current and historic times, Surowiecki first makes the case for diverse application of collective intelligence by showing the reader the best of what it can accomplish and the amazement of its accuracy.

The Wisdom of Crowds was a widely popular book and has since

> **"** This intelligence, or what I'll call 'the wisdom of crowds,' is at work in the world in many. **"**
> James Surowiecki, *The Wisdom of Crowds.*

gained international importance. The range of interest and applicability is huge; *The New York Times* Sunday Times describes it as, "A handsome addition to the books that combine the verve of smart magazine writing with a whiff of academia… a fantastically stylish counter to the expert-knows-best line… an offbeat argument for democracy…"[1] The text will continue to remain a relevant primer on the basics of collective wisdom and a source for creative application of the theory for years to come.

Author's Life

James Surowiecki was born in Meriden, Connecticut, in 1967. After spending several years of his childhood living in Puerto Rico, his family moved back to Connecticut and he graduated from Choate Rosemary Hall, a competitive preparatory boarding school in Wallingford, Connecticut, in 1988. He attended college at the University of North Carolina at Chapel Hill, where he was recognized as a Morehead Scholar, a prominent scholarship at UNC. Surowiecki then earned a PhD in American Studies at Yale University and was the recipient of a Mellon Fellowship.

Surowiecki pursued a career in journalism after the completion of his academic research. David Gardner, one of the founders of the *Motley Fool*, recruited Surowiecki to be the editor-in-chief for the company's online site, "Rogue." Gardner was a fellow UNC Chapel Hill graduate and, like Surowiecki, was a recipient of the Morehead Scholarship. After a year as the site's editor-in-chief, *Motley Fool* closed the site and transitioned to financial journalism. Surowiecki then began to focus on financial writing,* and wrote the Motley Fool's column in *Slate Magazine* from 1997 to 2000. Surowiecki continued to write for a number of popular magazines and journals, including *The New York Times*, *The New Yorker*, the *Wall Street Journal*, *Wired*, *New York Magazine*, *Fortune*, and the *MIT Technology Review*.[2]

In 2000, Surowiecki joined the editorial staff of *The New Yorker*, a popular American magazine that publishes articles on culture, fiction, satire, critiques, and is also popular for its graphical comics and caricatures. He wrote for "The Financial Page" and the "Currency Blog" for 17 years before parting with the publication in 2017 to pursue other projects, including future books. Prior to writing for *The New Yorker*, he wrote various articles for *Slate*, *Fortune*, and *Talk*.[3]

In 2002, Surowiecki edited his first book, *Best Business Crime Writing of the Year*, a collection of essays about the crimes committed by corporate CEOs and their subsequent downfall. His next book was *The Wisdom of Crowds*, published in 2004. He currently lives in Brooklyn, New York.

Author's Background

Surowiecki came of age during the "dot-com" bubble* of the late 1990s, a period of technological and economic frenzy that propelled America, and most of the modern world, into the age of the internet. Widespread use of the internet became commonplace, as did the ability to obtain knowledge and information from a variety of sources and connect with millions of individuals in new ways.[4] The dot-com bubble was a period of high-intensity growth in internet and data companies, such as Google, Yahoo Finance, America Online, Amazon, and other tech giants, as well as many, many smaller start-up companies. To claim market share and establish rapid growth, these companies often operated at a loss, masking the true financial circumstances for investors.[5]

The bubble had ripple effects in infrastructure upgrades, such as cell towers* and broadband communications infrastructure, as well as contributed more broadly to increases in consumer spending. In the early 2000s, however, due to over-spending and poorly executed mergers among media and internet giants, the bubble started to burst. Stock market indices fell more than seventy-five percent in the following years.[6] Surowiecki viewed the mania and madness of the investor crowds excited over the dot-com companies and their expected financial success with a critical eye, and his work outlines the criteria necessary to help individuals identify mania crowds before following their incorrect wisdom.

As a financial journalist* during this period, Surowiecki was well poised to remain intimately knowledgeable not just about current events in business, but also about the ways that information was shared and processed. In addition, the research and writing skills he developed as a journalist helped him connect his theories and ideas with a large and diverse audience.

NOTES

1   Review quote, *The New York Times,* https://www.bookdepository.com/Wisdom-Crowds-James-Surowiecki/9780349116051.

2   Contemporary Authors Online, The Gale Group, 2004, PEN (Permanent Entry Number): 0000156165.

3   Cision Media Research, "James Surowiecki Moves On," March 17, 2017, accessed November 7, 2017, https://www.cision.com/us/2017/03/james-surowiecki-moves-on/.

4   Floyd Norris, "The Year in the Markets: 1999: Extraordinary Winners and More Losers," *The New York Times*, January 3, 2000, accessed November 7, 2017, http://www.nytimes.com/2000/01/03/business/the-year-in-the-markets-1999-extraordinary-winners-and-more-losers.html.

5   Ironman. "Here's Why The Dot Com Bubble Began And Why It Popped," *Business Insider*, December 15, 2010. Accessed November 17, 2017, http://www.nasdaq.com/article/3-lessons-for-investors-from-the-tech-bubble-cm443106.

6   James K. Glassman, "3 Lessons for Investors from the Tech Bubble," *Kiplinger's Personal Finance*, February 11, 2015, accessed November 17, 2017, http://www.nasdaq.com/article/3-lessons-for-investors-from-the-tech-bubble-cm443106.

MODULE 2
ACADEMIC CONTEXT

KEY POINTS

- Business Management literature is concerned primarily with identifying ways that companies can be more productive and ways that managers can better identify and achieve goals.

- The internet has made it possible to aggregate large collections of data, opinions, and predictions.

- As a financial journalist, Surowiecki is knowledgeable about ways that organizations can benefit from insightful crowd knowledge.

The Work in its Context

The science of collective intelligence was thought to have originated as jury theory,* first explored by Marquis de Condorcet* in 1785. De Condorcet was a political scientist who explored the probability of a jury in reaching the correct verdict in his book, *Essay on the Application of Analysis to the Probability of Majority Decisions.* His work assumed that each juror was more likely than not to conclude the verdict correctly on his own, so that each additional juror added to the jury would subsequently improve the likelihood that the jury vote would select the correct verdict.[1] Sir Francis Galton* contributed to this field in 1906 with his statistical modeling of estimates for the weight of a butchered ox at a livestock fair, the most similar example of Surowiecki's specific argument about the "wisdom" of crowds.

Galton, however, made no mention as to the value of the crowd as a source for knowledge or insight. This link was made first by Douglas Engelbart* in 1962 in his paper "Augmenting Human Intellect: A

> ❝ It's an adventure story, a manifesto, and the most brilliant book on business, society and everyday life that I've read in years. ❞
>
> Malcolm Gladwell, review excerpt on book cover, *The Wisdom of Crowds*, by James Surowiecki

Conceptual Framework," where he outlined benefits of team cooperation. Engelbart later went on to become one of the leaders in the field of human-computer interaction and, in 1994, coined the term "collective IQ"* to describe the augmenting of intelligence by adding additional members to a group.[2]

While Surowiecki did not invent the concept of collective intelligence, he is credited with reintroducing the topic to the contemporary public in his book, *The Wisdom of Crowds*, which also straddles the fields of business management, economics, and psychology, and to an extent, popular culture.

Overview of the Field

The concept of "collective wisdom" refers to the idea that "two heads are better than one" when it comes to judging, making decisions, or generating knowledge and arguments. The claim is not new: in a well-known *Politics* passage, Aristotle* suggests "the many are better judges" than the individual in political and aesthetic affairs, because their judgment is informed by all the diversely competent members.[3] Centuries later, Condorcet's jury theorem* and the "miracle of aggregation"* lent credence to the idea that under the right conditions, the more numerous a group, the more likely it is to make the right decision."[4] Pierre Levy echoed many of Engelbart's ideas in his 1997 book *Collective Intelligence*, which speaks to the ways that shared knowledge across the internet would help advance mankind.

He identifies a "knowledge space" provided in cyberspace where knowledge can be aggregated and accessed by the masses.[5]

Surowiecki loosely draws on the works of Henry David Thoreau* and Frederich Nitzsche* and their thoughts about collective wisdom and the behavior and madness of large groups. The prevailing thought at the time was that individual knowledge and reason was reduced, not augmented, by an individual's participation in a crowd. In quoting Thoreau that "The mass never comes up to the standard of its best member but, on the contrary, degrades itself to a level with the lowest,"[6] Surowiecki is highlighting the long-standing bias toward the need for experts in making important decisions and how "Groups make people dumb, crazy, or both."[7]

Academic Influences

Somewhat ironically, some of the sources and influences Surowiecki references most heavily are those he seeks to disprove. He titled his book *The Wisdom of Crowds* in reference to *Extraordinary Popular Delusions and the Madness of Crowds*, by Charles MacKay* in 1841. This book describes crowd psychology and in particular, the ease by which individuals are led astray by groups of collective opinion. McKay, according to Surowiecki, would have "scoffed" at the idea of crowds knowing anything,[8] as his book popularized the idea of the "herd mentality," or "The tendency for people's behavior or beliefs to conform to those of the group to which they belong."[9] The term references the herd behavior of animals such as honeybees, cattle, or geese. McKay references popular and memorable examples such as "Tulipomania"* in seventeenth century Holland, and the witch hunts* in sixteenth- and seventeenth-century Europe.[10]

The democratization of knowledge, and subsequently of decision-making power by the democracy, builds off of the scholarship of collective wisdom. In 1895, French philosopher Gustave Le Bon* published *The Crowd: A Study of the Popular Mind*. In this book, he denounced the onset of democracy in the West and his disapproval of the political and decision-making power being transferred from landed aristocracy to merchants and businessmen.

NOTES

1   Reid Hastie and Kameda Tatsuya, "The robust beauty of majority rules in group decisions," *Psychological review 112*, no. 2 (2005): 494.

2   Douglas C. Engelbart, "Toward augmenting the human intellect and boosting our collective IQ," *Communications of the ACM 38*, no. 8 (1995): 30-32.

3   Juliette Roussin, "The Wisdom of Crowds, review of *Collective Wisdom: Principles and Mechanisms,*" trans. Michael C. Behrent. *Books and Ideas. net*. February 20, 2014. Accessed November 12, 2017, http://www. booksandideas.net/The-Wisdom-of-Crowds.html.

4   Roussin, "The Wisdom of Crowds," http://www.booksandideas.net/The-Wisdom-of-Crowds.html.

5   Pierre Levy, *Collective Intelligence*, (New York: Plenum/Harper Collins, 1997)

6   James Surowiecki, *The Wisdom of Crowds*, (New York: Anchor Books, 2004), xx.

7   CMX, "James Surowiecki: The Power of the Collective," YouTube video, 23:11, https://www.youtube.com/watch?v=pTI6u_gbilY.

8   Surowiecki, *The Wisdom of Crowds*, xv.

9   Oxford English Dictionary, 2017.

10   Adam Holownia, "Extraordinary Popular Delusions and the Madness of Crowds by Charles Mackay," Medium.com, February 8, 2017, https://medium.com/@obtaineudaimonia/extraordinary-popular-delusions-and-the-madness-of-crowds-by-charles-mackay-a0b8a2debc18.

MODULE 3
THE PROBLEM

KEY POINTS

- Scientists, programmers, and business leaders all look to aggregated knowledge as a potential source of information and prediction.

- Other experts fear the mass hysteria or madness component of crowd-sourced knowledge and warn against mimicking a crowd.

- Surowiecki helped navigate this topic by identifying the characteristics necessary for sound crowd knowledge and avoiding manias.

Core Question

There are two general opinions of crowd knowledge. One, that the crowd is easily influenced by hysteria, mania, or madness and often mimics or follows without proper consideration, largely because the crowd is made up of uneducated, non-experts who lack the proper training to determine the best course of actions. Galton and MacKay emphasize this view.[1] The other is the opposite: that the crowd follows the "two heads are better than one" mantra and that the aggregation of information is superior to the knowledge of any one individual, regardless of one's level of expertise.[2]

The Wisdom of Crowds explores the idea and power of "the collective." The book outlines the criteria necessary for a crowd to be wise, rather than foolish or manic. It identifies the types of problems well suited to crowd knowledge and how and why, under these carefully crafted circumstances, crowd knowledge can be superior to even the smartest of experts.

> ❝ Although it may be counter to our intuitions, the masses can be smarter than the solitary expert. So much for mediocrity. ❞
>
> Richard Adams, "The Jellybean Democracy," review in The Guardian

James Surowiecki's theories are not entirely original, and the book very briefly highlights the historic scholars, such as Condorcet, MacKay, and Galton, who explored similar questions and the events that shaped their exploration. Surowiecki adds additional depth by outlining the factors that take a crowd from wise to unwise by explaining how crowds can become manic. In 2002, management consultant Karl Albright introduced his "Albright's Law," which states: "Intelligent people, when assembled into an organization, will tend toward collective stupidity." He identifies two kinds of collective stupidity: "learned" kind, where individuals are not authorized to think, and "designed in" kind, where rules or policies make it impossible to achieve creative and independent thought.[3] Surowiecki addresses both kinds by explaining the importance of the criteria of wise crowds, including the need for independent and diversity of thought.

The Participants

Surowiecki opens *The Wisdom of Crowds* with a story about Sir Francis Galton,* an English statistician from the Victorian era* and also a cousin of evolutionary scientist Charles Darwin.* Since Surowiecki's work was published, Galton has since become colloquially known as the "father of modern collective intelligence." Galton was a firm believer in eugenics* and its application to humanity. In 1906, Galton attended a fair where the attendees entered a contest to guess the weight of an ox. Galton obtained the ox weight guesses from the fair administrators and developed statistical models for the data. His goal was to show how incorrect the crowd of common people was, what he learned from his analysis, however, was that, while no one person was correct, the average of the crowd's guesses was almost perfectly exact. Galton had disproven himself but had also proven an important theory on the wisdom of crowds and the power of the aggregation of data.[4]

The title of Surowiecki's book, *The Wisdom of Crowds*, is a spoof on *Extraordinary Popular Delusions and the Madness of Crowds*, a book published in 1841 by Scottish scientist Charles Mackay.* Mackay cautioned against the foolishness that can overcome the public, drawing on examples such as economic bubbles, alchemy, witch mania, and the role of religion and politics in influencing the public toward incorrect and even impossible conclusions.[5]

In the early 2000s, the emerging field of network science grew immensely, influencing the fields of physics, mathematics, computer science, biology, economics, and sociology, and access to the internet allowed for numerous applications. Scholarship in this field, however, is highly technical and computational in nature, beyond Surowiecki's text or the historical references he includes.[6] A particular branch of network science relevant to Surowiecki's theory is social contagion,* a popular topic of scientific and sociological literature in the early 2000s.

The Contemporary Debate

While the debate over the intelligence or foolishness of crowds has engaged statisticians and philosophers for centuries, Surowiecki makes the theory relevant to contemporary business leaders by applying it to organizational decision-making strategy. Surowiecki contends that, under the specific set of circumstances he outlines in the second half of *The Wisdom of Crowds*, that the intelligence of the "crowd" the members of an organization can be more useful, and often less costly, than the opinions or recommendations of a few chosen elite experts. Several articles from the *Harvard Business Review*, one of the top management publications in the United States, have confirmed Surowiecki's theory in application.

It is impossible to discuss Surowiecki's work in contemporary context without mentioning Scott Page's* 2008 work, *The Difference: How the Power of Diversity Creates Better Groups, Firms, Schools, and Societies.* In this book, Page dives into the idea of cognitive diversity,* one of Surowiecki's requirements for wise crowds, making the case that, "Diversity among a group of problem solvers is more important than individual excellence." This refers to the concept that when a group or team is assembled to solve a problem, it is most important to forma cognitively diverse team. For example, when addressing a legal issue, include members of the team that have no legal background, such as scientists, engineers or historical scholars.[7]

Likewise, scholarly articles in economics, political science, computer science, and biology that reference crowd wisdom are too numerous to count. Because there are so many nuanced applications for the application of this general theory, there are just as many variations on it, but the majority of literature on the subject follows a logical arc. It describes the application to a particular problem or topic, discusses the nuanced details required to address the specific details of the problem, and tests and quantifies the outcome, much in the same way Surowiecki describes the ox weighing game or the jelly bean counting exercise.

NOTES

1   Charles Mackay, *Extraordinary Popular Delusions,* (West Conshohocken, PA: Templeton Press, 2015; James Surowiecki, The Wisdom of Crowds, (New York: Anchor Books, 2004).

2   Alison Reynolds and David Lewis, "Teams Solve Problems Faster When They're More Cognitively Diverse," *Harvard Business Review*, March 30, 2017, https://hbr.org/2017/03/teams-solve-problems-faster-when-theyre-more-cognitively-diverse; Dave Roos, "No Wisdom in Crowds? One Head May Be Better Than Two or 22," HowStuffWorks.com, July 8, 2016, https://health.howstuffworks.com/mental-health/human-nature/behavior/no-wisdom-crowds-one-head-may-be-better-two-22.htm.

3   Karl Albrecht, *The Power of Minds at Work: Organizational Intelligence in Action. (New York: AMACOM Div American Mgmt Assn, 2003).*

4   John Kay, "The Parable of the Ox," *Financial Times*, July 24, 2012, accessed November 10, 2017, https://www.ft.com/content/bfb7e6b8-d57b-11e1-af40-00144feabdc0.

5   Richard Adams, "The Jellybean Democracy," *The Guardian*, August 6, 2004, accessed November 9, 2017, https://www.theguardian.com/books/2004/aug/07/highereducation.news2.

6   James Heskett, "Should the Wisdom of Crowds Influence Our Thinking About Leadership?" *Harvard Business Review*, October 31, 2004, https://hbswk.hbs.edu/item/should-the-wisdom-of-crowds-influence-our-thinking-about-leadership.; Alison Reynolds and David Lewis, "Teams Solve Problems Faster When They're More Cognitively Diverse," Harvard Business Review, March 30, 2017, accessed December 2, 2017, https://hbr.org/2017/03/teams-solve-problems-faster-when-theyre-more-cognitively-diverse.

7   Kenneth J. Arrow, "Review excerpt on book cover," *The Difference*, (Princeton: Princeton University Press, 2008).

THE AUTHOR'S CONTRIBUTION

KEY POINTS

- Surowiecki draws on multiple real-world examples to prove the immense knowledge available in diverse crowds.

- His work has helped develop applications for crowd knowledge to contribute to a wide range of problems.

- Surowiecki adds to historic theories on crowd knowledge by clarifying the criteria necessary for crowd wisdom to be accurate and relevant.

Author's Aims

James Surowiecki's main goal in *The Wisdom of Crowds* was to bring to modern light the centuries old theory of collective intelligence.* He was wildly successful in this aim, especially due to his fluid and captivating use of historic and present-day case study examples. Surowiecki also intended *The Wisdom of Crowds* to be a primer for leaders looking to apply this concept to decision-making within their own organizations. After priming readers on the theory and showcasing examples of application, Surowiecki provides the criterion he deems necessary for the theory to work in practice and gives examples of the type of problems this theory is best suited for. His ultimate aim is to show leaders how they can gain better insight, at less cost, by employing the collective knowledge of their own organization rather than chasing after and paying a heavy premium for expert knowledge.

Throughout the text, Surowiecki aims to engage the reader and impress him/her with the broad and powerful applications of collective wisdom. He aims to make this book as much of a fun read, as it is an

> **❝** He lays out a valuable counter-argument to the contempt for the crowd that dates back to the Victorian era. **❞**
>
> Richard Adams, "The Jellybean Democracy," review in *The Guardian*

educational one; his experience as a seasoned magazine writer helps accomplish this. By connecting with the readers in this way, Surowiecki helps ensure that his other aims are achieved and the impact is retained.

Approach

Surowiecki is a fabulous storyteller and puts his skills to good use throughout the book. *The Wisdom of Crowds* opens with a story, connecting readers with the power of collective intelligence and aggregated knowledge before introducing them by name. And his efforts on this aspect of writing are not wasted, as the book was widely recognized as much for what it said as for how it said it. As Joseph Nocera stated in his book, "Surowiecki has done the near impossible. He's taken what in other hands would be a dense and difficult subject and given us a book that is engaging, surprising, and utterly persuasive."[1]

Surowiecki helps convey the importance and pervasiveness of collective wisdom by showing readers how it is already at work in their everyday lives. For example, he highlights the example of the Google search engine, which uses a version of collective knowledge to establish its ranking system that provides search results. He also highlights the television game show *Who Wants to be a Millionaire?* When contestants were given the opportunity to use one of three types of "lifelines" to help them answer trivia questions, the option of polling the audience proved a more strategic choice than asking an expert. Asking the audience usually turned out to be a better choice due to the wide range of question categories and the fact that the "experts" available to be called were typically either celebrities or former contestants. Thus, there was a much higher chance that audience members, who were able to quickly converse before answering, would arrive at the correct answer.

To a large extent, the book follows the same approach Surowiecki has become famous for in his magazine articles. Surowiecki weaves these literary devices seamlessly into the more academic components of the book and does so in a way that makes them equally interesting as stories, making the book as enjoyable to serious readers as it is to causal ones. "There's no danger of dumbing down for the masses who read this singular book."[2]

Contribution in Context

Surowiecki is not alone ether in his focus on collective wisdom or in his use of "boundless erudition and delightfully clear prose."[3] Surowiecki's work is one of several popular books on a family of similar topics, written in similar form for both the business guru and the educated causal reader. The most notable contemporary peer author is Malcolm Gladwell,* famous for popular books such as *The Tipping Point*, *Blink*, and *Outliers*.

The "father" of collective knowledge is often considered to be Sir Francis Galton, and Surowiecki gives him due credit in his opening chapter. In addition to Galton, Surowiecki draws on a number of research experts, mainly economists, to support his theory. But he does this in a way that makes the reading experience very different from reading the research studies themselves, as he brings them together in fluid, clear ways and shows the overall trends in the exploration and application of this topic.

In addition to Malcolm Gladwell, Surowiecki's peer writers often include Steven Pinker,* Noam Chomsky,* Scott Page,* Stephen J. Dubner,* and Steven Levitt,* all of whom write on the application of economics and statistics and their application to real world examples via easily read, non-academic texts.

SECTION 2
IDEAS

MAIN IDEAS

KEY POINTS

- Surowiecki describes the ways in which collective intelligence is used to solve a variety of real-world problems.

- The main argument of *The Wisdom of Crowds* is that, under the right conditions, crowds are more intelligent than experts.

- Crowd intelligence is dependent upon a set of general characteristics and the types of problems that require thoughtful solutions.

Key Themes

The main idea of *The Wisdom of Crowds* is that the collective intelligence and decision-making power of aggregated groups of individuals can be equal to, if not greater than, experts. James Surowiecki explores this idea through multiple examples of its application in historic and recent times, including the development of the Linux* open-source programming language, the investigation of the Space Shuttle *Challenger* explosion,* and the search for the USS *Scorpion*, a nuclear submarine lost in mysterious circumstances during the 1960s.* In each of these case study examples, Surowiecki highlights the unique and impressive use of crowd wisdom as critical to solving the problem.

Surowiecki then identifies the three main types of problems that lend themselves well to collective wisdom solutions: cognition problems,* problems that have a definitive solution; cooperation problems,* problems that require individuals to put aside their self-

> " Under the right circumstances, groups are remarkably intelligent, and are often smarter than the smartest people in them. "
>
> James Surowiecki, *The Wisdom of Crowds*

interest; and coordination problems,* problems that require groups of strangers to work together. He also identifies the necessary characteristic for a crowd to be wise, rather than foolish, and how one can tell the difference.

A major theme for Surowiecki is that experts are not necessary, and that leaders need not look any further than their own organization for a source of knowledge and insight. Surowiecki sets the argument that one expert, no matter how intelligent and savvy, can never replicate the cognitive diversity of a crowd that meets the critical conditions outlined in his book. "Intelligence alone is not enough, because intelligence alone cannot guarantee you different perspectives on a problem. Adding in a few people who know less, but have different skills, actually improves the group's performance."[1]

Finally, *The Wisdom of Crowds* sets up the reader to be a savvy generator of crowd knowledge. Surowiecki provides the reader with specifics suggestions on the ways in which, for example, survey questions can be customized to solicit crowd-based wisdom appropriate for aggregation and drawing collective conclusions.

Exploring the Ideas

Surowiecki identifies several characteristics of crowds that must be met before one can harness their full collective power and avoid following a "foolish" crowd. The first is decentralization, in which power, organization, or rule making is shifted from a central authority and dispersed amongst individual members, which is required for individuals to draw on local knowledge. The second, and most important characteristic is diversity, specifically cognitive diversity, which ensures that individuals are approaching the problem or question from different angles. Sociological diversity, such as race, gender, age, nationality, religion, or other social/demographic characteristics may help contribute to cognitive diversity, but it is not nearly as important as true cognitive diversity, which comes from differences in training, education, personality, or mental thought processes. Achieving true cognitive diversity, however, can be a challenge, and Surowiecki notes that organizations tend to be self-selective or inherently selective by necessity.[2]

The third characteristic is independence of thought. Individual actors must not be strongly influenced by other group members. This can be simply achieved by a secret ballot polling situation or by limiting or preventing interaction among group members while working toward a solution. This helps ensure that individuals are relying on their own judgment and not relying on the work done by others or are acquiescing to peer pressure to confirm or support other's conclusions. Surowiecki deems this a paradox; a crowd is collectively most intelligent when the individuals in it are acting as independently as possible. The final characteristic is aggregation, as the collective wisdom of individuals means nothing before it is combined in a meaningful way. Crowd wisdom offers nothing if the opinions of the masses have no way of being brought together to signify the true opinion of the entire crowd.

Language and Expression

Surowiecki's writing is accessible to anyone and strikes a solid balance of engaging the general public as equally as subject matter experts. Surowiecki is passionate about the potential of the theory of collective intelligence and successfully conveys this to the reader. His story-telling ability goes hand in hand with his use of case study examples, which combine to make his ideas memorable and applicable.

Surowiecki makes some very broad claims and ones that are likely to be criticized by others, but takes care to provide numerous examples to back up his viewpoints.[3]

Fluid, engaging language is a hallmark of Surowiecki's full portfolio of work, and is evident in *The Wisdom of Crowds*. Because of his background and training in magazine and editorial-style writing, Surowiecki excels in the story-telling component of the work and helps create anticipation and enthusiasm for what could otherwise be a somewhat mundane topic. Surowiecki uses his skill in storytelling to organize the book, beginning each chapter with a unique story that illustrates the application of his crowd intelligence theory on a variety of real life examples. According to author Michael Vaughn in his review of the book, *The Wisdom of Crowds* is an enjoyable read with an engaging style, similar to reading a series of magazine articles. Vaughn was particularly impressed that every chapter or section begins with a hook to keep readers interested.[4]

NOTES

1   James Surowiecki, *The Wisdom of Crowds*, (New York: Anchor Books, 2004), 30.

2   Surowiecki, *The Wisdom of Crowds*.

3   Pamela Jones, "Groklaw Review of "The Wisdom of Crowds," November 7, 2004, accessed November 17, 2018, http://www.groklaw.net/articlebasic. php?story=20041107180408325, para. 3.

4   Michael Vaughn, *Book review, 'The Wisdom of Crowds' by James Surowiecki*, YouTube video, 4:37, October 7, 2009, https://www.youtube. com/watch?v=hF8LdUSmyB4.

MODULE 6
SECONDARY IDEAS

KEY POINTS

- The main secondary idea in *The Wisdom of Crowds* is the importance of cognitive diversity within groups or organizations.

- Surowiecki notes that cognitive diversity is important in business, government, academia, and research institutions.

- Surowiecki provides practical recommendations for achieving cognitive diversity within different types of groups.

Other Ideas

One of James Surowiecki's biggest supporting themes is the importance of diversity, specifically cognitive diversity, and how to achieve it within a group or organization. Cognitive diversity is the "differences in perspective or information processing styles. It is not predicted by factors such as gender, ethnicity, or age."[1] Non-experts, according to Surowiecki, add value simply because they think about a problem in different ways. This can help prevent the group from making the same mistakes over and over, and from failing to consider non-traditional or innovative solutions. Surowiecki is adamant that even those group members who have no direct knowledge on a topic can, in the right circumstances, add value simply by thinking about the problem in a different way.

As James himself put it at the 2016 CMX Summit, "Even if you know less you can actually add value, as long as what you know is different."[2] One of the best ways to add cognitive diversity to an

❝ The argument of this book is that chasing the expert is a mistake, and a costly one at that. ❞
James Surowiecki, *The Wisdom of Crowds*

organization is by adding new members. New members can add tremendous value because they typically need to ask a number of questions as they learn about the organization and the problem. By asking questions, even mundane questions, new members can prompt group veterans to reconsider information they thought was unimportant.

Equally important as to what makes a crowd intelligent is the inverse what makes a crowd foolish. Surowiecki identifies several characteristics of "foolish" crowds. The first is too much sharing. "Paradoxically, the best way for a group to be smart is for each person in it to think and act as independently as possible."[3]

Exploring the Ideas

Surowiecki identifies three types of problems that can be successfully and appropriately addressed with crowd intelligence: cognition problems, coordination problems, and cooperation problems. Cognition problems are defined as problems that have, or will have, definitive solutions, such as which team will win a sporting event or which candidate will win an election, or questions of probability, likelihood, or best fit.[4]

The second kind of problem is a coordination problem. Coordination problems are situations or environments where unrelated members of a group, sometimes without any formal or direct communication, must figure out how to interact with one another, often when formal rules have been suspended, such as when a traffic signal is not working properly. The standard rules for interaction cannot be followed, and if no traffic cop is there to direct traffic, individuals have to determine how to coordinate their activities so as not to cause accidents.[5]

The third type of problem is a cooperation problem, where self-interested independent individuals must work together, trust each other, and contribute toward the common good when it is often in their own self-interest not to. Cooperation problems are akin to the "Tragedy of the Commons,"* a classic environmental problem that explains how early American settlers must all limit the grazing of their sheep to sustain the town green. Surowiecki provides examples of coordination problems such as paying taxes, dealing with pollution, and agreeing on definitions of what counts as reasonable pay.[6]

Overlooked

The final section of *The Wisdom of Crowds* highlights a few examples when the crowd is not wise, nor is the idea of following it, such as riots or stock market bubbles. As noted by Sabine Hossenfelder in his review of the book, "Surowiecki warns of factors that dumb down the decisions of groups, most notably skewing information, groupthink, and herding, all of which lead to suboptimal decisions, and potentially disastrous failures."[7] These situations are labeled as the extremes of collective behavior and Surowiecki identifies two types of behavioral "traps" that aggregated groups can fall subject to: mimicking and herd behaviors. Mimicking behavior happens when individuals all collect around a single conclusion, either because they are uncertain of their own opinion, feel pressure to conform, fear retribution from dissent, or merely to expedite the resolution. Herd behavior occurs when the group inherently moves in a single direction, much like an animal herd, without centralized direction.

Although much of the book is devoted to how the crowd can outsmart the expert, Surowiecki also explains why experts, while knowledgeable, can oftentimes offer less than crowd-aggregated results. This is because the experts in a given field are likely all trained in similar ways and will go about solving a problem in a similar fashion. Truly hard problems are those that typically cannot be solved in traditional ways. The introduction of cognitive diversity within a group, however, pushes the expert to think outside her normal ways and consider new approaches. From an organizational perspective, one of the best sources of cognitive diversity is often the group's newest member.

NOTES

1   Alison Reynolds and David Lewis, "Teams Solve Problems Faster When They're More Cognitively Diverse," *Harvard Business Review*, March 30, 2017, accessed December 2, 2017. https://hbr.org/2017/03/teams-solve-problems-faster-when-theyre-more-cognitively-diverse, para. 5.

2   CMX Summit 2016, "James Surowiecki: The Power of the Collective," YouTube video, 23:11, CMX Summit 2016, "James Surowiecki: The Power of the Collective," YouTube video, 23:11, https://www.youtube.com/watch?v=pTl6u_gbilY.

3   James Surowiecki, *The Wisdom of Crowds*, (New York: Anchor Books, 2004), xix.

4   Surowiecki, *The Wisdom of Crowds*, xvi.

5   Surowiecki, *The Wisdom of Crowds*, xviii.

6   Surowiecki, *The Wisdom of Crowds*, xviii.

7   Sabine Hossenfelder, "Book Review: *The Wisdom of Crowds,*" by James Surowiecki," *Back Reaction*, July 28, 2009, accessed December 2, 2017, http://backreaction.blogspot.com/2009/07/book-review-wisdom-of-crowds-by-james.html, para. 5.

MODULE 7
ACHIEVEMENT

KEY POINTS

- *The Wisdom of Crowds* represents Surowiecki's most notable work to date.

- The success of *The Wisdom of Crowds* was partly due to Surowiecki's established readership at *The New Yorker*.

- Some critics argued that Surowiecki's theory was self-limiting due to the extensive requirements for application.

Assessing the Argument

In *The Wisdom of Crowds,* James Surowiecki assesses the current state and potential impact of crowd knowledge. While these concepts are not new, Surowiecki's work is unique for several reasons. First, his use of case study examples helps the reader associate the concept with real-world applications. Two, his development of criteria for use and application is critical to the soundness of the concept overall, and three, his fluid, witty writing style makes the concept accessible and interesting to readers. Surowiecki's established readership in popular magazines helped the book gain popularity. As stated by *Bookforum* on the book's cover jacket, *The Wisdom of Crowds* is "Clever and surprising... The originality and sheer number of demonstrations of the impressive power of collective thinking provided here are fascinating, and oddly comforting."[1]

The Wisdom of Crowds' careful description of the criteria necessary for collective knowledge to provide accurate and meaningful insight is one of the main aspects that distinguishes Surowiecki's work from other texts on the topic. These criteria are important both to those who read the book simply for educational and entertainment purposes,

> **❝** Collective intelligence. Think of how Wikipedia works, how Amazon harnesses user annotation on its site, the way photo-sharing sites like Flickr are bleeding out into other applications. **❞**
>
> Tim O'Reilly, *Time Magazine*

as it provides insight into the theory's application, and also to those who wish to apply it to their own organizations. Surowiecki cautions that the application of collective knowledge without ensuring these criteria are met is not something he advocates for or recommends.

The concepts brought to light in *The Wisdom of Crowds* have inspired numerous subsequent works on the subject and its myriad applications and have prompted debate on the value of "expert" wisdom. One of the most notable extensions of Surowiecki's book is Scott Page's *The Difference: How the Power of Diversity Creates Better Groups, Firms, Schools, and Societies.* Page, an American social scientist and professor of economics and political science at the University of Michigan, builds directly off of Surowiecki's work by detailing a nuanced exploration of cognitive diversity.

Achievement in Context

By the time he published *The Wisdom of Crowds*, Surowiecki had already established himself as a prominent magazine journalist specializing in financial reporting. The range of his argument, and its application, have helped the book gain popularity, but have also opened it up to criticism from scholars in numerous fields. Kenneth Arrow, in his review, notes that, "Surowiecki ranges across fields as diverse as popular culture, psychology, the biology of ants, behavioral economics, artificial intelligence, military history, and politics to show how this simple idea offers important lessons for how we live our lives, select our leaders, run our companies, and think about our world."[2]

While the book and the concept have become popular, Surowiecki has faced criticism, primarily due to the over-simplification of the idea of "crowd wisdom" and because the criteria he describes is so specific as to make it almost unattainable. Ken Arrow again notes, "It has become increasingly recognized that the average opinion of groups is frequently more accurate than most individuals in the group. The author has written a most interesting survey of the many studies in this area and discussed the limits as well as the achievements of self-organization."[3]

The popularity of *The Wisdom of Crowds* is due to the wide range of its subject matter, as well as the wide range of readership, much of which had already been established during Surowiecki's day job as a popular magazine writer and columnist; all of which led to several re-releases since initial publication in 2004.

Limitations

Surowiecki is self-limiting in his ideas about crowd wisdom. Many of his critiques center on the extensive requirements for true crowd intelligence and its applicability of use. It is hard to imagine a situation in which all Surowiecki's requirements are met. Eric Klinenberg, in his review of the book, expands on this theme, stating, "Surowiecki's case for the crowd is ultimately unpersuasive, largely because his theory suggests that the conditions that foster collective wisdom are hard to come by, and his research turns up so many examples where groups go awry... Surowiecki recognizes that much of what we call history is the story of groups making big and consequential mistakes. He claims that four key conditions characterize wise crowds diversity of opinion, independence, decentralization and aggregation and shows that there is trouble when any one condition is absent."[4]

Others question the value of crowd knowledge in the examples he gives. His defining case study, where the public tries to guess the weight of an ox at a livestock fair, is amusing, but that knowledge is easily obtained simply by putting the ox meat on a scale. The jellybean example, another crowd estimation problem, follows suit: guessing the jellybeans makes for a fun activity but provides society with little value. For Surowiecki's theory to be truly impressive, it must be both accurate and add value to society, otherwise it is little more than a novelty.

NOTES

1   Book Forum, "Review excerpt on book cover," *The Wisdom of Crowds* by James Surowiecki, (New York: Anchor Books, 2004).

2   Book Forum, Review excerpt on book cover, *The Wisdom of Crowds* by James Surowiecki, Anchor Books, 2004.

3   Kenneth Arrow, Review excerpt on book cover, *The Wisdom of Crowds* by James Surowiecki, (New York: Anchor Books, 2004).

4   Eric Klinenberg, "Strength in Numbers, review of *The Wisdom of Crowds,*" *The Washington Post*, September 7, 2004, accessed December 2, 2017, http://www.washingtonpost.com/wp-dyn/articles/A1355-2004Sep6.html.

MODULE 8
PLACE IN THE AUTHOR'S WORK

KEY POINTS

- Surowiecki is an established and popular financial journalist who writes for some of America's most notable publications.

- As the most recent book published by Surowiecki, it is difficult to predict its relationship with the future of his career.

- While Surowiecki was already an established name in financial journalism, *The Wisdom of Crowds* significantly broadened his readership.

Positioning

James Surowiecki had already published some of the content in *The Wisdom of Crowds* previously in his columns, as collective knowledge is a topic he gradually developed an interest in. He first explored the topic as an extension of his writings about the stock markets. Surowiecki had noticed that investors, even some extremely skilled investors, rarely could outperform the stock market. The stock market, he concluded, was one of the biggest agglomerations of crowd knowledge, in contrast with economic theories of rational actors and perfect information. Time and again, research for his articles showed him different examples of how mostly ordinary people had come together to solve complex problems.[1]

The Wisdom of Crowds represents, thus far, the culmination of Surowiecki's career. By the time it was published in 2004, Surowiecki was already a well-established financial journalist who published regular columns in some of America's most popular and widely-read

> 66 Businesses have started to use 'crowdsourcing' for a diverse range of tasks that they find can be better completed by members of a crowd rather than by their own employees. 99
>
> Paul Whitla, "Crowdsourcing and its Application in Marketing Activities."

magazines. It is easy to see the elements of Surowiecki's background come together in this book his PhD in American studies primes him well for developing relevant case studies, while his extensive experience in financial journalism helps him communicate quantitative academic concepts to a wide range of readers. Furthermore, Surowiecki's lack of formal academic training in economics keeps him focused on the practical, real-world happenings and prevents him from delving too far into economic theory.

Integration

Surowiecki has spent the majority of his professional life exploring the concepts of finance, economics, and current events, and communicating these conceps to wide and diverse audiences. While there is a definitive and recognizable arc to his collective body of work, *The Wisdom of Crowds* represents a departure from the financial columns that made him a recognizable name in financial journalism. While some of his articles are seemingly unrelated, several articles near the time *The Wisdom of Crowds* was published highlighted some of the main concepts in the book such as "Mass Intelligence," published in Forbes on May 24, 2004. The article described the PageRank algorithm developed by Google, which relies on many of the same crowd-wisdom principles Surowiecki describes in his book. Other articles, such as his 2007 article "Crowdsourcing the Crystal Ball" on prediction markets, also published in Forbes, follow similar themes. Like all his work, it is a smooth, interesting read.

According to Scott McLemee in his review of the work, "The author has a knack for translating the most algebraic of research papers into bright expository prose."[2]

Reviewers are quick to note that Surowiecki is, at heart, grounded in his financial upbringing. McLemee also notes, "Surowiecki's framework is decidedly capitalist.* The market is a mechanism for translating 'the wisdom of crowds' into optimal results, though things would probably improve if business leaders were a little less prone to thinking that, as Margaret Thatcher* once put it, 'There is no such thing as society.' Whether Surowiecki's book will prevent another Enron* is very much to be doubted, but his worldview is at least less cynical than Victorian notions that humanity, as a group, is a dumb herd."[3]

Surowiecki's corpus of articles could be seen as a whole, albeit maybe a disjointed one. However, the disjointed quality comes not from the author but from the topics, which although most are related to finance, vary greatly in their specific focus. Surowiecki's years of financial reporting are most cohesive when viewed as his evolving perspective on the current financial events of the time.

Significance

The Wisdom of Crowds marks a turning point for Surowiecki. It is the first book the author has written in entirety. His prior book, *Best Business Crime Writing of the Year*, was an anthology of previously published essays written by other authors and edited by Surowiecki. While it is difficult to say whether or not *The Wisdom of Crowds* is Surowiecki's most important work, it is certain that it has done significant things for his career. The book transformed Surowiecki from a notable journalist into a widely recognized author. Even though the book has garnered its share of criticism, it remains a popular work and Surowiecki's career has continued to prosper. As of December 1, 2017, the book ranks number thirteen on Amazon's Best Seller list in Social Theory, fifty-second in Consumer Behavior, and seventy–eighth in Economic History.

Surowiecki's recent announcement of departure from *The New Yorker*[4] will no doubt be a disappointment to his devoted readers. His statement for leaving said he was "...going to be working on a book [or books], and looking for other interesting projects." On the heels of the success of his first book, it is likely that Surowiecki will continue to captivate his readers with insight, passion, and superb storytelling just as he did in *The Wisdom of Crowds*.

NOTES

1   Big Think Interview with James Surowiecki, *Big Think*, YouTube video, 59:13, April 23, 2012, accessed December 1, 2017 https://www.youtube.com/watch?v=afIRcqXN8ZA.

2   Scott McLemee, Book review: "The Wisdom of Crowds': Problem Solving Is a Team Sport,' *The New York Times*, May 22, 2004, accessed December 2, 2017, http://www.nytimes.com/2004/05/22/books/review/the-wisdom-of-crowds-problem-solving-is-a-team-sport.html, para. 2.

3   McLemee, 2004

4   Roush, Chris. "Surowiecki leaves *The New Yorker*," *Talking Biz News*, March 11, 2017, accessed November 7, 2017, http://talkingbiznews.com/1/surowiecki-leaves-the-new-yorker.

SECTION 3
IMPACT

THE FIRST RESPONSES

KEY POINTS

- Initial reactions to *The Wisdom of Crowds* were mixed; some lauded the book while others poked holes in Surowiecki's theory.
- Surowiecki has clarified the book's uses and applicability in subsequent speaking engagements and interviews.
- The most important critique on Surowiecki's crowd intelligence theory is whether the required criteria are too limiting to make it practically useful.

Criticism

Many lauded James Surowiecki's book, *The Wisdom of Crowds,* as a witty, entertaining addition to the relatively new trend toward pseudo-academic books from peers like Malcolm Gladwell, Stephen J. Dubner, Steven Levitt, and Daniel Kahneman* that focused on the everyday application of economic or statistical theories to real-world examples. The book brought Surowiecki to a new level of recognition as an author who, according to a Denver Post book review, was "… a patient and vivid writer with a knack for telling examples."[1]

However, the book also attracted criticism. One of the main critiques of *The Wisdom of Crowds* is that Surowiecki's theories only hold true under very specific, limiting circumstances. As journalist Michael Vaughn states, "he puts so, so many conditions on what makes a crowd have wisdom that it really doesn't have anything to do with crowds it requires a perfect assembly of people working in perfect conditions."[2] Others have criticized the depth of Surowiecki's theory

> ❝ In an age routinely denouncaed as selfishly individualistic, it's curious that a great deal of faith still seems to lie with the judgement of the crowd. ❞
>
> Philip Ball, "Wisdom of the Crowd: Myths and Realities"

and argument, stating that the book illustrates situations that prove little more than the power of averages.[3]

It is easy to find counter-examples to Surowiecki's theory, such as investment bubbles and popular scientific theories later disproven, and critics have wondered how these unwise crowds are fundamentally different than the ones that Surowiecki characterizes. Surowiecki is quick to note that these crazed crowds of investors don't meet the criteria he outlines, but his critics note that the long list of required conditions essentially makes the application almost impossible and thus practically useless. As one critic noted, "I like the stories better than I like the theories."[4]

Responses

After publication, Surowiecki remained closely associated with, and engaged with the book. One of the most common ways Surowiecki responds to criticism is to remind readers to actually read the whole book and carefully consider the criteria and conditions he sets forth later in the book, in addition to the attention-catching case study examples. Many readers, it seems, focus on the case studies and then look to find other examples that disprove Surowiecki's theory without considering the criteria he outlines later in the book. This is also noted by Ilan Mochari,* who states, "As with most concepts that become popular, there's a gap between the actual concept and what most people believe is the concept." [5]

Surowiecki has been challenged on the practicality of his theory. Given Surowiecki's extensive criterion, some critics wonder if intelligent crowds actually exist.[6] Surowiecki's response is that the point of the book is not to send readers out looking for intelligent crowds already in existence, but to give them the tools and insights to create a wise crowd. Creating a wise crowd, argues Surowiecki, can be an extremely savvy way for organization leaders to source amazing amounts of knowledge toward better decision-making.

The Wisdom of Crowds was published in 2004, just as social media was about to take off. Applications of collective wisdom within the realm of social media have exploded since Surowiecki announced his theories to the world. In 2009, book reviewer Michael Vaughn summarized the some of the advancements that build off of Surowiecki's theory on collective intelligence.[7] He mentions two books, *Wikinomics: How Mass Collaboration Changes Everything,* by Anthony D. Williams,* which outlines the huge and successful collaboration that can take place online, and *Super Crunchers: Why Thinking-by-Numbers Is the New Way to be Smart,* by Ian Ayres,* which explores data-based decision making rather than just crowd aggregation. Both, according to Vaughn, have not disproven Surowiecki's theory, but have done a much better job of explaining the nuances of this type of thinking. Surowiecki, states Vaughn, does a great job of reporting, but often stretches the case studies to fit into his theory. Kirk McElhearn* concurs, noting "[It] seemed like Surowiecki was trying to push a lot of square pegs into round holes to confirm his theory."[8]

Conflict and Consensus

Surowiecki and his critics all agree that under the right conditions, crowds can be equally, if not more intelligent, than experts; however, like many things, the devil is in the details. As the range of application for collective knowledge grows, there will continue to be new debates over how to apply the theory to emerging fields, and how valuable this type of problem solving and knowledge sourcing* can be. It is not appropriate to say that either the author or the critics have changed their position or convinced one another of their error, but that the debate continues to explore the basic ideas in new ways. These debates are the same today as they were when the book was published more than a decade ago, and it is likely that the debate will remain characterized that way for years to come.

The afterword of the 2005 edition speaks to this point. Surowiecki highlights his increased popularity in the months following the book's first publication and how he was asked over and over again to lead estimation contests similar to the ox's weight guessing contest. Each time he ran a contest or experiment, the results would prove his theory to be true. These iterations, however, are in line with the criteria for wise crowds, and the problem is relatively simple. The types of applications where Surowiecki's critics find the holes are those that he shies away from.

NOTES

1   Denver Post, "Review excerpt on book cover," *The Wisdom of Crowds* by James Surowiecki, (New York: Anchor Books, 2004).

2   Michael Vaughn, *Book review, The Wisdom of Crowds by James Surowiecki*, YouTube video, 4:37, October 7, 2009, accessed November 30, 2017, https://www.youtube.com/watch?v=hF8LdUSmyB4; Ilan Mochari, "Challenging the Wisdom of Crowds," *INC*, May 16, 2014, accessed December 2, 2017, https://www.inc.com/ilan-mochari/wisdom-crowds-challenging.html.

3   Cass R. Stunstein, *Infotopia: How many minds produce knowledge*, (Oxford University Press, 2016).

4   Dave Roos, "No Wisdom in Crowds? One Head May Be Better Than Two or 22," *HowStuffWorks,com*, July 8, 2016, accessed November 28, 2017 https://health.howstuffworks.com/mental-health/human-nature/behavior/no-wisdom-crowds-one-head-may-be-better-two-22.htm, para. 4.

5   Ilan Mochari, "Challenging the Wisdom of Crowds," *INC*, May 16, 2014, https://www.inc.com/ilan-mochari/wisdom-crowds-challenging.html.

6   Michael Vaughn, "Book review, *The Wisdom of Crowds* by James
    Surowiecki," YouTube video, 4:37, October 7, 2009, accessed November
    30, 2017, https://www.youtube.com/watch?v=hF8LdUSmyB4; Ilan Mochari,
    "Challenging the Wisdom of Crowds," *INC*, May 16, 2014, accessed
    December 2, 2017, https://www.inc.com/ilan-mochari/wisdom-crowds-
    challenging.html.

7   Vaughn, *The Wisdom of Crowds by James Surowiecki*.

8   Kirk McElhearn, "Technology and Society, review of *The Wisdom of Crowds*,"
    TechSoc,com, November 8, 2017, accessed November 15, 2017, http://
    www.techsoc.com/wisdomofcrowds.htm, para. 4.

THE EVOLVING DEBATE

KEY POINTS

- Surowiecki's theory on the accuracy of collective wisdom, under perfect circumstances, was largely accepted.
- The debate shifted to focus on refining the criteria for use within numerous fields.
- Though not exactly the same, collective knowledge and the "wisdom of crowds" have come to be used interchangeably.

Uses and Problems

Many aspects of our modern society are being democratized: navigation, finance, transportation, even fine cuisine. Included in this list are perhaps the two most important: information and knowledge. Wikipedia, the open-source programming and software platform James Surowiecki highlights as a model of crowd wisdom, is highly convenient and is decisively increasing access to basic knowledge worldwide; however, it is often also simply wrong, displaying both factual and incorrect information in the same article and in the same format, leaving readers with little guidance on how to tell the difference.[1] This trend is augmented with the proliferation of social media and the integration of social media and news media. It can often be difficult for readers to identify the source of information and assess its validity.

Much of the subsequent work that builds off of Surowiecki's text is highly computational in nature and the discussions often focus on the adjustment of small details in the modeling of knowledge aggregation. Many of the articles that build off of Surowiecki's work apply his

> ❝ It may be, in the end, that a good society is defined more by how people treat strangers than by how they treat those they know. ❞
>
> James Surowiecki, *The Wisdom of Crowds*

concepts to advanced mathematical, statistical, or economic problems, such as the modeling of stock market predictions, or the influence of other factors in determining crowd accuracy, or the behavior of herding animal populations. Although these research findings and their comments on Surowiecki's presentation of crowd intelligence theory are significant in establishing the importance of *The Wisdom of Crowds*, it is difficult to discuss this portion of the use of Surowiecki's argument outside of those subject-specific academic communities mentioned.

Schools of Thought

Surowiecki's book has not established a new school of thought; however, there are two main branches of scholarship that build off of *The Wisdom of Crowds*. One focuses on the development of some of the criterion established by Surowiecki, most commonly on cognitive diversity, and the other focuses on the ever-increasing examples of the application of collective knowledge. Within the latter, there is a sub-set that focuses heavily on applications related to the use of social media.

Scott Page, author of *The Difference: How the Power of Diversity Creates Better Groups, Firms, Schools, and Societies*, is one of the most notable scholars to extend the depth and range of Surowiecki's work on cognitive diversity. Cognitive diversity has become its own specific school of thought, and the debates focused on this idea remain tied back to Surowiecki's book. "Diversity, however, is not the pinnacle of optimal decision-making. No amount of diversity can help if the population is completely ignorant on a given issue, or if opinions are diverse, but heavily skewed. Thus, the composition of diversity is as important as diversity itself."[2]

Pavlin Mavrodiev* further elaborates on the impact of social influence on cognitive diversity. "We have demonstrated that groups whose initial average opinion is relatively far from the truth in general benefit from stronger social influence… The effect of social influence, however, is detrimental to groups with a relatively accurate initial configuration and thus suffer from an increased drift in the aggregated opinion…Finally, other initial conditions exist, where even traces of social influence leads to deterioration in the long-term collective error."[3]

In Current Scholarship

Surowiecki's aim in *The Wisdom of Crowds* is not one of intense computational or even scientific knowledge. It is one of familiarization with an old, but perhaps forgotten and discounted, idea about tapping the minds of the everyday people around us rather than searching for and rushing to the experts.

The debates outlined in previous sections continue to be the focus of current scholarship on the general topic: under the correct, near perfect conditions, the theory holds true, but determining in detail what describes the needed criteria and subsequently ensuring those conditions are met continues to be a challenge for scholars and leaders. For example, as Erik Klinenberg states in his review, "Markets, crowds, and democracies work well under the right conditions, and Surowiecki has identified them remarkably well. The trouble is that the right conditions are so difficult to produce and sustain. And… small bursts of collective stupidity can do permanent damage."[4] Additionally, the perceived accuracy of individual's level of expertise on the subject seems to matter. One study found that as participants received more information regarding a study topic, their guesses tended to narrow, and the collective conclusion actually moved *farther* from the correct value.[5] Another study points to the perceived level of information individuals think other crowd members may have. "Trouble starts, as Surowiecki readily concedes, when individuals start to adjust their first thoughts and reactions with what they think others are thinking, or when judgments are too little influenced by the diverse views of others."[6] In the field of land-use planning, Australian municipalities have taken Surowiecki's principles and applied them to participatory planning efforts with measurable success.[7]

The Wisdom of Crowds continues to be a popular general reference for subsequent work in the area of collective knowledge, but given the range of its application in current scholarship, it would be unlikely that Surowiecki would be engaged with all scholars who cite his work. Rather, Surowiecki remains engaged in highlighting the power of the idea and of highlighting some of the ways it is being applied to new areas of research.

NOTES

1   Aniket Kittur and Robert E. Kraut, "Harnessing the wisdom of crowds in Wikipedia: quality through coordination," Proceedings of the 2008 ACM conference on Computer supported cooperative work, (2008): 37-46, http://repository.cmu.edu/cgi/viewcontent.cgi?article=1098&context=hcii.

2   Eric Bonabeau, "Decisions 2.0: The power of collective intelligence," *MIT Sloan Management Review* 50, no. 2 (2009): 45, para 7.

3   Jan Lorenz, Heiko Rauhut, Frank Schweitzer, and Dirk Helbing, "How social influence can undermine the wisdom of crowd effect," *Proceedings of the National Academy of Sciences,* 108, no, 22 (2011): 9020-9025, November 12, 2017, http://www.pnas.org/content/108/22/9020.full.pdf; Pavlin Mavrodiev, Claudio J. Tessone, and Frank Schweitzer, "Effects of social influence on the wisdom of crowds," *arXiv preprint arXiv:1204.3463* (2012).

4   Eric Klinenberg, "Strength in Numbers, review of *The Wisdom of Crowds,*" *The Washington Post*, September 7, 2004, accessed November 20, 2017, http://www.washingtonpost.com/wp-dyn/articles/A1355-2004Sep6.html.

5   Philip Ball, "Wisdom of the Crowd: Myths and Realities," BBC, July 8, 2014, http://www.bbc.com/future/story/20140708-when-crowd-wisdom-goes-wrong.

6   Will Hutton, "The Crowd Knows Best," *The Observer*, September 18, 2005, accessed November 10, 2017, https://www.theguardian.com/observer/comment/story/0.6903.1572869.00.html.

7   Greg Brown, "Engaging the wisdom of crowds and public judgement for land use planning using public participation geographic information systems," *Australian Planner* 52, no. 3 (2015): 199-209.

MODULE 11
IMPACT AND INFLUENCE TODAY

KEY POINTS

- *The Wisdom of Crowds* remains an important, but often incorrectly criticized, book in management and decision science genres.

- Many find the text to be an incomplete guide to the application of crowd intelligence, or find it misused.

- Much of Surowiecki's speaking engagements since publication have focused on clarifying the theory and its requirements for application.

Position

James Surowiecki's *The Wisdom of Crowds,* remains a relevant work in both business and popular culture. It is often cited as the core modern text in this particular subject area, and the author is commonly credited for introducing this idea to the non-expert public. Google Scholar indicates the original 2005 publication has been cited more than 9,000 times[1] in articles with a wide range of subjects, from biology to stock market prediction to robotic intelligence.

Although the shortcomings of the text are clear, those shortcomings have been the source for the next phase of scholarship on crowd intelligence, and it is likely that Surowiecki, by bringing some of these shortcomings to light himself, has spurred research and innovation into the next phase of collective intelligence scholarship. Because it is a general primer on the topic of collective knowledge, *The Wisdom of Crowds* will likely remain an intriguing study about an idea.[2] It is still directly involved in debates over the uses and applications of collective knowledge today, in such diverse applications as statistical modeling,

> ❝ Crowdsourcing has also triggered a dramatic shift in the way work is organized, talent is employed, research is conducted, the products are made and marketed. ❞
>
> Jeff Howe, Crowdsourcing: How the Power of the Crowd is Driving the Future of Business.

computer programming, and assessing animal herd behavior, although the debates typically mention it as an introductory summary before moving on to more nuanced applications, which often point out some of the theory's shortcomings.

Interaction

The Wisdom of Crowds is still relevant to a number of different fields and to a broad range of quantitative problems. Surowiecki's text has continued to be applied to numerous fields of research and finds special resonance with internet-related problems. That is not surprising, as the internet is the world's largest "crowd." However, the last of Surowiecki's four criteria, aggregation, is an entire field within its own right, as algorithms that aggregate and make sense of data obtained from the internet continue to be a huge and growing field.

Recently, several articles highlighting the impacts of political affiliation[3] and bias within collective knowledge have surfaced, particularly regarding the 2016 United States presidential election,[*4] and the subsequent uprising of mob-like crowd behavior in the US. Such articles underscore the need to distinguish between wise and foolish crowds.

Several critics have questioned the extent to which Surowiecki's theories hold true. For example, Mirta Galesic,* a professor of social dynamics, has observed that many of the country's most important decisions are made by small groups. "A jury in most countries is six to 15 people and central bank boards are five to 12 people. If the wisdom of crowds is so important, why don't we make these groups much larger? Why don't we use the internet and online teleconferencing to have juries with 150 people? And how many economists do you need to most accurately predict macroeconomic shifts? Seven, which is precisely the number of seats on the Federal Reserve's* Board of Governors."[5]

The Continuing Debate

Both direct and indirect references to the book continue to appear in academic scholarship and popular culture. Surowiecki's text has even inspired a prime-time television drama in the United States, aptly titled "Wisdom of the Crowd," released in 2017. The plot follows a visionary technology inventor who creates a crowd-sourcing app to solve the case of his daughter's murder. In doing so, the protagonist revolutionizes modern crime solving and forensics in the process.

The value of crowd intelligence remains debated when questions cannot be verified by factual knowledge or the occurrence of predicted events. In further clarification of Surowiecki's identification of crowd source-appropriate questions, she notes, "not all questions are equal. First, the wisdom of crowds can only be tested using quantitative questions with a single right answer how many gumballs are in the jar? Or which of these two candidates will win the election? It doesn't work, for example, with juries, because you can never be sure if a verdict of innocent or guilty was ultimately right or wrong. Some guilty people really do get away with murder."[6]

An interesting application of crowd wisdom that embodies Surowiecki's criterion is the growing field of design competitions, which invite diverse teams of individuals to submit ideas or solutions to contemporary problems, often for monetary prizes.[7] Likewise, Surowiecki ends the afterword of the 2006 reprint by acknowledging the basic principle that, because one doesn't always know from where to get good information, casting a wide next is often the easiest and most foolproof strategy.[8]

NOTES

1   *Goo Google Scholar* search, January 15, 2018, scholar.google.com search "The Wisdom of Crowds."

2   CMX. "James Surowiecki: The Power of the Collective." YouTube video, 23:11. Posted June 13, 2016. Accessed December 1, 2017. https://www.youtube.com/watch?v=pTI6u_gbilY, time 0:56.

3   Daniel Cooper, "MIT Finds Actual Wisdom in the Wisdom of Crowds," *Engadget*, January 26, 2017, accessed November 24, 2017, https://www.engadget.com/2017/01/26/mit-finds-actual-wisdom-in-the-wisdom-of-crowds/.

4   Robert Zaretsky, "Donald Trump and the Myth of Mobocracy: How the Dubious Ideas of a 19th-century Frenchman Reverberate in 2016," *The Atlantic*, July 27, 2017, accessed November 24, 2017, https://www.theatlantic.com/international/archive/2016/07/trump-le-bon-mob/493118/.

5   Mirta Galesic et al., "Smaller Crowds Outperform Larger Crowds and Individuals in Realistic Task Conditions," Decisions (2016), DOI: 10.1037/dec0000059.

6   Mirta Galesic et al., "Smaller Crowds Outperform Larger Crowds and Individuals in Realistic Task Conditions," Decisions (2016), DOI: 10.1037/dec0000059.

7   Joseph Lampel and Pushkar Jha, "Test-Driving the Future," *The Academy of Management Perspectives* 26, no. 2 (2012): 71-85.

8   James Surowiecki, *The Wisdom of Crowds*, (New York: Anchor Books, 2006), 280.

WHERE NEXT?

KEY POINTS

- Given the ever-increasing importance of social media, big data,* and the internet, *The Wisdom of Crowds* will likely remain relevant for years.

- Surowiecki's criteria will help organization leaders capitalize on the knowledge available in crowds and put it to appropriate use.

- *The Wisdom of Crowds* sets the stage for the next generation of crowd-sourced data and problem solving.

Potential

Scholars and critics have been quick to respond to James Surowiecki's work in both a positive and negative light, but the response itself is indicative of the book's relevance. As decision science and "big data" become increasingly popular for myriad applications, references to Surowiecki's book will no doubt continue. Several areas are well poised for application of crowd intelligence, such as prediction markets* (markets that trade at a price based on the likelihood of an event occurring), Delphi methods* (forecasting methods based on asking question to a panel of experts), and human swarming* (where groups of online participants answer questions.) However, these applications all circle around similar themes, notably the quest for predicted factual answers that can be verified; questions on opinion, and applications of opinion polls, are less appropriate.

The Wisdom of Crowds is likely to be out-paced by subsequent research on data science and intelligence aggregation. In its most extreme replacement, artificial intelligence* may, in its own way,

> **❝** The idea holds so much appeal for the social software community that 'the wisdom of crowds' has become a part of the vernacular. **❞**
>
> Daniel Bayn, from his blog

partially replace Surowiecki's theories while simultaneously building upon them. Counting jellybeans, for example, may need no aggregation of knowledge by a robot, yet imagine hundreds of those same robots navigating the sidewalks of New York City, relying on much the same way of processing their environment as do the pedestrians Surowiecki so vividly describes.[1] Yet *The Wisdom of Crowds* will likely hold a place of its own in much the same way as does Galton's trip to the ox-weighing livestock fair: important, but perhaps nostalgic.

Future Directions
The future of crowd-based, big data, or aggregated research seems limitless. The internet continues to expand the way we can source, aggregate, and access data, while advances in math and computer programming continue to understand trends and predict outcomes. No doubt this will help to advance myriad fields, from health care to criminal investigation, and even aid in helping shoppers order more correctly-sized clothes from online retailers. However, the vulnerability of data, both public and personal, continues to present huge and ever-increasing risks. Surowiecki assumes the information provided by the crowd is truthful in its source, even if it is inaccurate. Advising one to capitalize on the power of collective knowledge, when that knowledge may itself have been tampered with, could have huge and serious consequences.

Critics warn against selective recollection of Surowiecki's work and fear the next generation of social media developers will quickly forget the circumstances Surowiecki so carefully outlines to preserve the integrity of crowd intelligence. Critics also warn against putting more value in crowd "wisdom" than it offers. Truly diverse (random) opinions will always vary around the mean. Aggregating lots of random observations or opinions can lead to a deceptively precise average, but this doesn't necessarily translate to "wisdom." Rather, it's more appropriately an effect of the Law of Large Numbers. Any hint of systematic bias will cause the whole theory to collapse.

Surowiecki cites many potential sources of bias in his book, and social software developers would be wise to take note. Social psychology offers many more: polarization, conformity, in-group bias, framing, groupthink, and so on. The real science deals with why groups are dumb.[2]

Summary

As the power of the internet and our ability to aggregate data continues to grow, *The Wisdom of Crowds* will likely remain a popular read. Surowiecki captures the power and amazement of the concept through the description of well-selected case studies. He grounds these descriptions with objective criteria that ensures best possible conclusions and then groups these criteria in two main categories: one, the types of problems best addressed with crowd intelligence, and two, the necessary characteristics to ensure the integrity of the knowledge provided by the crowd. The three types of problems that best lend themselves to crowd intelligence are cognition problems, cooperation problems, and coordination problems.[3] The four criteria for ensuring applicability of the theory are cognitive diversity, decentralization, individual independence, and aggregation methodology.[4]

Just as importantly, *The Wisdom of Crowds* speaks to its own limitations. It cautions the reader against widespread application of its theories to inappropriate problems and identifies the factors that predispose a crowd to hysteria, mania, or madness.[5] *The Wisdom of Crowds* has earned a place in popular culture as well as management theory, as other books, articles, and TV shows all reference its name. Surowiecki, despite confidence in his work, urges organization leaders, including corporate CEOs and governing officials to apply his theories cautiously. By tapping the intelligence of the organization rather than chasing an expert, Surowiecki purports that leaders will make better, cheaper, more relevant decisions about the future direction of their organizations.

NOTES

1   "The wisdom of crowds: The strange but extremely valuable science of how pedestrians behave," *The Economist,* December 17, 2011, accessed November 30, 2017, http://www.economist.com/node/21541709.

2   Jeff Howe, *Crowdsourcing: How the power pf tje crowd is driving future futue of business*, (new York: Random House, 2008).

3   James Surowiecki, *The Wisdom of Crowds*, (New York: Anchor Books, 2004), xx.

4   Surowiecki, *The Wisdom of Crowds*, xx.

5   Surowiecki, *The Wisdom of Crowds*, xx.

GLOSSARY

GLOSSARY OF TERMS

1984: a classic novel published in 1949 by English author George Orwell that describes a fictional future dystopian society that requires overwhelming conformism and monitors the thoughts of its citizens by "Thought Police."

2016 United States Presidential Election: highly controversial, partisan, and vitriolic election featuring candidates Hillary Clinton (D) and Donald J. Trump (R), in which Trump lost the popular vote but was ultimately elected.

Aggregation: the process of bringing a group of items or ideas together.

Artificial Intelligence (A.I.): the capability of a machine to imitate intelligent human behavior, such as speech recognition or decision-making.

Bay of Pigs Invasion (April 17, 1961): an attempted (but failed) military invasion of Communist Cuba by the United States.

Bayes' Theorem: statistical method for determining the probability of a future event occurring based on conditions related to the event and circumstances.

Big Data: computational analysis of enormous data sets to reveal trends or patterns. Typically focused on human behavior *(e.g., teen shopping habits)*.

Capitalist: economic system defined by investment and largely private ownership of the means of production and distribution.

Cell Towers: shortened form of cellular towers, a network of antennas used to transmit and receive signals from mobile telephones.

Cognition problems: problems involving mental impairments that may include memory loss or deficiencies in judgment, thinking, or learning capabilities that are classified as outside the normal range for one's peer group.

Cognitive Diversity: differences in thought patterns, information processing approaches, or perspectives within a group.

Collective Intelligence: shared intelligence arising from a combination of the shared efforts, individual competition amongst, and collaboration of large groups of people engaged in consensus decision-making. Used interchangeably with "collective IQ."

Collective Wisdom: general term used to describe the aggregation of individual knowledge within a group. Also called co-intelligence or collective wisdom.

Compendium of the Cacoethes: generalized, society-wide mania.

Cooperation Problems: problem involving the inability of a group of individuals to agree on and collectively work toward a shared goal in a coordinated fashion.

Coordination Problems: problem involving the inability of a group of individuals to manage individual inputs and work together effectively toward a shared goal.

Criminal Forensics: utilizing scientific techniques to aid in a criminal investigation, typically these techniques relate to collecting and analyzing physical or digital evidence.

Crowd Aggregation: the process of gathering immense amounts of data from various sources such as social media and discussion boards, to synthesize and draw insights.

Crowd Knowledge: knowledge that is aggregated from a large group of unrelated individuals.

Crowdsourcing: method of sourcing ideas, finances, or goods and services from a widespread and disparate group of internet users, such that everyone does a small piece to achieve an aggregated and cumulative result.

Crowd Wisdom: the combined, averaged answers of many people, thought to lead to, in some case, more accurate solutions than consulting experts.

The Crusades (1095–1291): six major military campaigns in medieval times that were driven by the Christian church, with the dual purpose of recapturing the Holy Land from Muslim rule and suppressing paganism and heresy.

Decentralization: a process by which power, organization, or rule-making is shifted from a central authority to a dispersed or scattered body.

Delphi method: forecasting method utilizing several rounds of anonymous questionnaires sent out to a panel of experts, the results of which are shared with the group after each round, with the goal of increasing forecast accuracy.

Dot-Com Bubble (1997–2001): a period of rapid financial growth related to the creation and booming growth of internet and communications companies.

Dot-Com Investors: individuals who invested in new technology and web-based companies during the dot-com bubble, expecting unusually high returns. Many suffered significant financial loss when the bubble burst.

El Farol Bar Problem: Game Theory prediction problem regarding the optimal attendance at a small bar in Santa Fe, New Mexico, developed by W. Brian Arthur, an economics professor at Stanford University.

Enron: enormously successful energy company that misstated earnings, defrauded investors, and collapsed into financial ruin almost overnight in 2001.

Eugenics: is the concept of selectively choosing genetic traits to groom and modify future generations of the human population.

Federal Reserve: central bank of the United States. Provides the United States with a stable monetary and financial system and sets US monetary policy.

Financial Journalist: person who reports on current, business-related events, such as mergers and acquisitions, dividends, IPO's, or other events impacting financial markets.

Financial Writing: creation of articles, books, or other publications that comment on current events, business news, or broader corporate trends that are of interest to investors or impact financial markets.

FutureMAP Policy Analysis Market (PAM): a futures exchange program developed by DARPA (United States Defense Advanced Research Projects Agency).

Green Revolution: a period of agricultural development in India in the late 1960s that increased crop yields through modern farming practices and technology applications.

Herding: the practice of a group moving or reacting together as a single unit rather than as a group of individuals.

Human Swarming: process by which individuals leverage unified collective intelligence and work cooperatively in real-time to answer questions or make predictions, often with extremely accurate results.

Information Cascade: a mathematical model of information distribution where a person or actor observes a behavior and then replicates that behavior.

Iowa Electronic Markets Project: a prediction market founded at the Iowa College of Business in 1988 that uses real money to predict major political elections in the United States.

Jury Theory: theory first advanced by Marquis de Condercet, positing that each individual juror was more likely than not to arrive at the correct verdict in a trial, and that each additional juror would therefore improve the likelihood that the jury vote would ultimately select the correct verdict.

Knowledge Aggregation: process of gathering large amounts of information and data from many sources.

Knowledge Sourcing: process by which individuals seeking expertise or knowledge on a topic can connect with subject-matter experts using a variety of avenues.

Linux: a free and open-source operating system that builds off the Linux kernel developed by Finnish hacker Linus Torvalds in 1991.

Mania: a form of mental illness in which a person exhibits exuberance, overactivity, extreme euphoria and overconfidence, and other delusions.

Miracle of Aggregation: idea by Marquis de Condercet that groups using a majority vote to reach a decision are more likely to reach a correct decision, even if each individual is only slightly more likely than chance to do so.

Opinion Aggregation: another term for crowd intelligence *(see above)*.

(Attack on) Pearl Harbor (December 7, 1941): was a surprise military attack by Japan on the United States Naval base at Pearl Harbor, Hawaii, which prompted the United States to enter World War II.

Plank Road Fever: The term coined to describe the fury of plank road construction in the late 1840s as part of an overall phase of infrastructure development in the southern United States.

Prediction Market: an exchange-traded market that uses a market price to predict the probability of an event occurring based on the crowd's opinion.

Risk Assessment: evaluating potential risks in a systematic manner prior to beginning a project or activity and establishing mitigation strategies.

Social Contagion: the likelihood of behavior being copied or mimicked either by those who are in local proximity or those who are informed of the behavior in media outlets.

South Sea Bubble: occurred in the early eighteenth century, when the South Sea Company, a joint-stock partnership created to consolidate and drive down the cost of Great Britain's national debt, became severely overvalued by investors as it expanded, until its financial collapse in 1720.

Space Shuttle *Challenger* disaster (January 28, 1986): US space shuttle exploded 73 seconds after takeoff from Cape Canaveral, Florida, killing all the members of the crew. The disaster was the product of a failure of the O-Ring seal on a fuel tank.

Tacit Knowledge: a type of knowledge that is difficult to transfer or communicate from one person to another, such as the ability to speak a language or play a musical instrument.

Tragedy of the Commons: economic theory that requires everyone to act in the interest of the group for mutual group and self-benefit.

Tulipomania (Dutch Tulip Mania): refers to a market bubble that took place in seventeenth-century Holland, in which tulips were significantly overvalued, leading to rampant over-speculation by casual investors and financial ruin for many.

Unix: a group of computer programming and software languages characterized by modular design begun around the 1970s.

USS *Scorpion*: a US submarine sunk in June of 1968. The lost boat was located utilizing naval resources as well as public analyses and efforts to find the wreck.

Victorian era weight-guessing game: game played during livestock fairs, in which a barker would engage passersby and guess their weight.

Victorian Era: period of Queen Victoria's reign in the United Kingdom (1837 – 1901); it was defined by a growing interest in mysticism and romanticism.

Witch Hunts: generalized moral panic in Europe (and later America) from the sixteenth to the eighteenth centuries that certain women were witches, leading to many executions.

"Who Wants to Be a Millionaire?": a quiz-format American game show that originally aired between 1999 and 2002. Contestants were asked successively more difficult multiple-choice questions for the chance to win $1 million.

PEOPLE MENTIONED IN THE TEXT

Aristotle (384–322 BC): Greek philosopher and scientist whose extensive writings on a wide variety of subjects formed the basis of the first Western philosophical system.

W. Brian Arthur (1946–present): English-American economist who is noted for the theory of increasing returns and created the El Farol Bar problem in 1994.

Ian Ayres (1959–present): prominent and prolific writer, economist, and lawyer who has taught at many top universities and is considered one of the world's leading legal scholars.

Bernard Baruch (1870–1965): American investor, speculator, and political consultant who was a financial advisor to US Presidents Woodrow Wilson and Franklin Delano Roosevelt.

William Beebe (1877–1962): American naturalist and former director of the New York Zoological Society.

George W. Bush (1946–present): Forty-third president of the United States who served in office from 2001 to 2009 and was also the former Governor of Texas.

Fidel Castro (1926–2016): Communist leader of Cuba from 1959 to 2008.

Avram Noam Chomsky (1928–present): American linguist, scientist, and philosopher credited with being the father of linguistics

Marquis de Condorcet (1743-1794): French mathematician and philosopher who created an analytical method to select the winning candidate in elections.

John P. Craven (1924-2015): American naval scientist who successfully applied the Bayesian search theory to locating the USS Scorpion.

Charles Darwin (1809-1882): Scientist who created the theory of evolution based on natural selection, published in his seminal work, *On the Origin of Species*.

General William Donovan (1883-1959): American soldier and military intelligence scholar who led the Office of Strategic Services, the predecessor to the Central Intelligence Agency (CIA), during World War II.

Stephen J. Dubner (1963-present): American journalist and author, most famous for co-authoring the book *Freakonomics: A Rogue Economist Explores the Hidden Side of Everything*.

Thomas Edison (1847-1931): American inventor and businessman who is credited with several notable inventions, including the light bulb, phonograph, and motion picture camera, and holds 1,093 US patents.

Douglas Engelbart (1925-2013): American inventor and engineer who founded the field of human-computer interaction (HCI). He theorized that the rate of human performance grows exponentially, known as Engelbart's Law.

Henry Ford (1863-1947): American industrialist and businessman who founded the Ford Motor Company in 1903.

Mirta Galesic (living): professor at Sante Fe Institute who researches cognitive biases, social judgments, collective performance, and group decision strategies and how humans cope with the uncertainty in everyday decisions.

Francis Galton (1822–1911): British scientist, statistician, inventor, and meteorologist who published more than 300 books and was knighted in 1909.

Malcolm Gladwell (1963–present): English-born Canadian author and staff writer for *The New Yorker* who published *The Tipping Point: How Little Things Can Make a Big Difference* in 2000.

Norman L. Johnson (1917-2004): American professor of statistics and probability theory who taught at the University of North Carolina at Chapel Hill.

Steven Johnson (1968-present): American author who published the book *Emergence: The Connected Lives of Ants, Brains, Cities, and Software* in 2001.

Daniel Kahneman (1934-present): Nobel prize-winning Israeli-American psychologist known for his work on decision-making, judgment, and behavioral economics.

John Kerry (1943-present): American politician from the Democratic Party who served as the US Secretary of State from 2013 to 2017.

John Maynard Keynes (1883-1946): American economist and author of *The General Theory of Employment, Interest, and Money*, published in 1936.

Richard Larrick (living): American professor at the Fuqua School of Business at Duke University whose research focuses on energy, development, and the global environment.

Gustave Le Bon (1841-1931): was a French writer who published *The Crowd: A Study of the Popular Mind* in 1895.

Steven Levitt (1967-present): American economist most famous for co-authoring the book *Freakonomics: A Rogue Economist Explores the Hidden Side of Everything.*

Charles Mackay (1814-1889): Scottish journalist who published the *Extraordinary Popular Decisions and the Madness of Crowds,* one of the earliest studies of crowd philosophy, in 1841.

Michael T. Maloney (1949-present): American economist and former financial professor who participated in the investigation of the *Challenger* explosion.

Pavlin Mavrodiev (living): professor at ETH Zurich who researches social influence and team productivity on social media platforms, such as Twitter and Facebook.

Kirk McElhearn (living): freelance writer and author who frequently writes for online periodicals and websites, such as MacWorld and TechSoc.

Ilan Mochari (living): writer and poet known for challenging the concepts in *The Wisdom of Crowds.*

J. Harold Mulherin (living): American finance professor at the University of Georgia who was heavily engaged with research on the *Challenger* Space Shuttle crash investigation.

Friedrich Nietzsche (1844–1900): German philosopher who developed extensive scholarship on Western Philosophy and Existentialism.

Ransom E. Olds (1864–1950): American businessman who founded the Oldsmobile and REO automotive corporations.

Scott E. Page (1963–present): American sociology professor at the University of Michigan and author of *The Difference: How the Power of Diversity Creates Better Groups, Firms, Schools, and Societies,* published in 2007.

Steven Pinker (1954–present): Canadian-American linguist and cognitive psychologist who researches psycholinguistics and visual cognition.

Richard Shelby (1934–present): United States Senator from Alabama (D) who is currently serving his sixth term.

Jack B. Soll (living): American sociologist and professor at the Fuqua School of Business at Duke University whose research focuses on the psychology of judgment and decision-making.

Margaret Thatcher (1925–2013): first woman to be appointed British Prime Minister and served from 1979 to 1990. Known for conservative, resolute political views and uncompromising style of interaction.

Henry David Thoreau (1817–1862): American philosopher, naturalist, and leader of the transcendentalist movement, who published *Walden* in 1854.

Jack Treynor (1930–2016): American finance professor who served as the former editor of the *Journal of Investment Management*.

William H. Whyte (1917–1999): American author and urbanist who published *The Organization Man* in 1956.

Anthony D. Williams (1974–present): researcher and consultant most widely known for co-authoring the book *Wikinomics: How Mass Collaboration Changes Everything*

WORKS CITED

WORKS CITED

Review quote, *New York Times*, Accessed November 12, 2017. https://www.bookdepository.com/Wisdom-Crowds-James-Surowiecki/9780349116051.

"The wisdom of crowds: The strange but extremely valuable science of how pedestrians behave." *The Economist.* December 17, 2011. Accessed November 12, 2017. http://www.economist.com/node/21541709.

"Weddings: Meghan O'Rourke, James Surowiecki." *The New York Times*. July 22, 2007. Accessed November 10, 2017. http://www.nytimes.com/2007/07/22/fashion/weddings/22orourke.html.

Adams, Richard. "The Jellybean Democracy," review of *The Wisdom of Crowds*, by James Surowiecki. *The Guardian*. August 6, 2004. Accessed November 10, 2017. https://www.theguardian.com/books/2004/aug/07/highereducation.news2.

Albrecht, Karl. *The power of minds at work: Organizational intelligence in action*. New York: AMACOM Div American Mgmt Assn, 2003.

Arrow, Kenneth J. Review excerpt on book cover, *The Difference*, by Scott Page. Princeton University Press, 2008.

Ball, Philip. "Wisdom of the Crowd: Myths and Realities." *BBC*. July 8, 2014. Accessed November 10, 2017. http://www.bbc.com/future/story/20140708-when-crowd-wisdom-goes-wrong.

Cooper, Daniel. "MIT Finds Actual Wisdom in the Wisdom of Crowds." *Engadget*. January 26, 2017. Accessed December 5, 2017. https://www.engadget.com/2017/01/26/mit-finds-actual-wisdom-in-the-wisdom-of-crowds/.

Daniel Bayn, "On the Wisdom of Crowds: Social software developers should remember the many caveats of Surowiecki's theory," *danielbayn.com*. Accessed November 18, 2017 http://danielbayn.com/on-the-wisdom-of-crowds/.

"Big Think Interview with James Surowiecki." *Big Think*. YouTube video, 59:13, April 23, 2012. Accessed November 10, 2017. https://www.youtube.com/watch?v=afIRcqXN8ZA.

Brown, Greg. "Engaging the wisdom of crowds and public judgment for land use planning using public participation geographic information systems." *Australian Planner* 52, no. 3 (2015): 199-209.

Bonabeau, Eric. "Decisions 2.0: The power of collective intelligence." *MIT Sloan management review* 50, no. 2 (2009): 45.

Book Forum. Review excerpt on book cover, *The Wisdom of Crowds* by James

Surowiecki. Anchor Books, 2004.

Collins, Rod. *Review excerpt on book cover. The Wisdom of Crowds,* by James Surowiecki. Anchor Books, 2004.

Contemporary Authors Online. The Gale Group, 2004. PEN (Permanent Entry Number): 0000156165.

CMX. "James Surowiecki: The Power of the Collective." YouTube video, 23:11. Posted June 13, 2016. Accessed December 1, 2017. https://www.youtube.com/watch?v=pTl6u_gbilY.

"Do crowds make better decisions than individuals? Yes, says author James Surowiecki in The Wisdom of Crowds," *Decision Science News*, September 12, 2004. Accessed December 5, 2017. http://www.decisionsciencenews.com/2004/09/12/do-crowds-make-better-decisions-than-individuals-yes-says-author-james-surowiecki-in-the-wisdom-of-crowds/.

Denver Post. Review excerpt on book cover, *The Wisdom of Crowds* by James Surowiecki. Anchor Books, 2004.

Engelbart, Douglas C. "Augmenting human intellect: a conceptual framework (1962)." *PACKER, Randall and JORDAN, Ken. Multimedia. From Wagner to Virtual Reality. New York: WW Norton & Company* (2001): 64-90.

"Toward augmenting the human intellect and boosting our collective IQ." Communications of the ACM 38, no. 8 (1995): 30-32.

Entertainment Weekly. Review excerpt on book cover, *The Wisdom of Crowds* by James Surowiecki. Anchor Books, 2004.

Glassman, James K. "3 Lessons for Investors From the Tech Bubble." *Kiplinger's Personal Finance*. February 11, 2015. Accessed December 7, 2017. http://www.nasdaq.com/article/3-lessons-for-investors-from-the-tech-bubble-cm443106.

Hastie, Reid, and Tatsuya Kameda. "The robust beauty of majority rules in group decisions." *Psychological review* 112, no. 2 (2005): 494.

Heskett, James. "Should the Wisdom of Crowds Influence Our Thinking About Leadership?" *Harvard Business Review*. October 31, 2004. Accessed December 7, 2017. https://hbswk.hbs.edu/item/should-the-wisdom-of-crowds-influence-our-thinking-about-leadership.

Holownia, Adam. "Extraordinary Popular Delusions and the Madness of Crowds by Charles Mackay," *Medium.com*, February 8, 2017. Accessed November 12, 2017. https://medium.com/@obtaineudaimonia/extraordinary-popular-delusions-and-the-madness-of-crowds-by-charles-mackay-a0b8a2debc18.

Hossenfelder, Sabine. "Book Review: *The Wisdom of Crowds*", by James Surowiecki." *Back Reaction*. July 28, 2009. Accessed November 12, 2017.

http://backreaction.blogspot.com/2009/07/book-review-wisdom-of-crowds-by-james.html.

Hutton, Will. "The Crowd Knows Best." *The Observer*. September 18, 2005. Accessed November 11, 2017. https://www.theguardian.com/observer/comment/story/0,6903,1572869,00.html.

Ironman. "Here's Why The Dot Com Bubble Began And Why It Popped." *Business Insider*. December 15, 2010. Accessed December 7, 2017. http://www.nasdaq.com/article/3-lessons-for-investors-from-the-tech-bubble-cm443106.

Jones, Pamela. "Groklaw Review of "The Wisdom of Crowds." November 7, 2004. Accessed November 12, 2017. http://www.groklaw.net/articlebasic.php?story=20041107180408325, para. 3.

Kay, John. "The Parable of the Ox." *Financial Times*. July 24, 2012. Accessed December 8, 2017. https://www.ft.com/content/bfb7e6b8-d57b-11e1-af40-00144feabdc0.

Kittur, Aniket and Kraut, Robert E. "Harnessing the wisdom of crowds in Wikipedia: quality through coordination." *Proceedings of the 2008 ACM conference on Computer supported cooperative work*, (2008): 37-46. Accessed November 12, 2017. http://repository.cmu.edu/cgi/viewcontent.cgi?article=1098&context=hcii.

Klinenberg, Eric. "Strength in Numbers, review of 'The Wisdom of Crowds'." *The Washington Post*. September 7, 2004. Accessed December 17, 2017. http://www.washingtonpost.com/wp-dyn/articles/A1355-2004Sep6.html.

Lampel, Joseph, Pushkar P. Jha, and Ajay Bhalla. "Test-driving the future: How design competitions are changing innovation." *The Academy of Management Perspectives* 26, no. 2 (2012): 71-85.

Mackay, Charles. *Extraordinary popular delusions*. West Conshohocken, PA: Templeton Foundation Press, 2015.

McElhearn, Kirk. Book review: "Technology and Society," review of *The Wisdom of Crowds*." *TechSoc.com*. Accessed November 8, 2017. http://www.techsoc.com/wisdomofcrowds.htm.

McLeemee, Scott. "The Wisdom of Crowds': Problem Solving Is a Team Sport," Review of The Wisdom of Crowds. *The New York Times*. May 22, 2004. Accessed November 5, 2017. http://www.nytimes.com/2004/05/22/books/review/the-wisdom-of-crowds-problem-solving-is-a-team-sport.html.

Mavrodiev, Pavlin, Claudio J. Tessone, and Frank Schweitzer. "Effects of social influence on the wisdom of crowds." *arXiv preprint arXiv:1204.3463* (2012).

Mochari, Ilan. "Challenging the Wisdom of Crowds." *INC*. May 16, 2014.

Accessed November 9, 2017. https://www.inc.com/ilan-mochari/wisdom-crowds-challenging.html.

Nocera, Joseph. Review excerpt on book cover, *The Wisdom of Crowds* by James Surowiecki. Anchor Books, 2004.

Norris, Floyd. "THE YEAR IN THE MARKETS: 1999: Extraordinary Winners and More Losers". *New York Times. January 3, 2000. Accessed December 2, 2017.* http://www.nytimes.com/2000/01/03/business/the-year-in-the-markets-1999-extraordinary-winners-and-more-losers.html.

Lévy, Pierre. *Collective intelligence*. New York: Plenum/Harper Collins, 1997.

Lorenz, Jan, Heiko Rauhut, Frank Schweitzer, and Dirk Helbing. "How social influence can undermine the wisdom of crowd effect." *Proceedings of the National Academy of Sciences,* 108, no. 22 (2011): 9020-9025. Accessed November 12, 2017. http://www.pnas.org/content/108/22/9020.full.pdf.

Review excerpt on book cover, *The Wisdom of Crowds* by James Surowiecki. Anchor Books, 2004.

Reynolds, Alison and Lewis, David. "Teams Solve Problems Faster When They're More Cognitively Diverse." *Harvard Business Review*. March 30, 2017. Accessed December 2, 2017. https://hbr.org/2017/03/teams-solve-problems-faster-when-theyre-more-cognitively-diverse.

Roos, Dave. "No Wisdom in Crowds? One Head May Be Better Than Two or 22." *HowStuffWorks.com*. July 8, 2016. Accessed December 7, 2017. https://health.howstuffworks.com/mental-health/human-nature/behavior/no-wisdom-crowds-one-head-may-be-better-two-22.htm.

Rosenberg, Louis. "Artificial Swarm Intelligence, a Human-in-the-loop approach to AI." In *AAAI*, pp. 4381-4382. 2016.

Roush, Chris. "Surowiecki leaves The New Yorker." *Talking Biz News*. November, 2017. Accessed November 11, 2017. http://talkingbiznews.com/1/surowiecki-leaves-the-new-yorker/.

Roussin, Juliette. "The Wisdom of Crowds, review of *Collective Wisdom: Principles and Mechanisms,*" trans. Michael C. Behrent. *Books and Ideas. net*. February 20, 2014. Accessed November 12, 2017. http://www.booksandideas.net/The-Wisdom-of-Crowds.html.

Surowiecki, James. *The Wisdom of Crowds*. New York: Anchor Books, 2004.

Vaughn, Michael. "Book review. "The Wisdom of Crowds" by James Surowiecki." YouTube video, 4:37. Posted October 7, 2009. https://www.youtube.com/watch?v=hF8LdUSmyB4.

Watts, Duncan J. "The "new" science of networks." *Annu. Rev. Sociol.* 30

(2004): 243-270. http://www.annualreviews.org/doi/abs/10.1146/annurev.
soc.30.020404.104342

Zaretsky, Robert. "Donald Trump and the Myth of Mobocracy: How the Dubious
Ideas of a 19th-century Frenchman Reverberate in 2016." *The Atlantic*,
July 27, 2017. Accessed December 2, 2017. https://www.theatlantic.com/
international/archive/2016/07/trump-le-bon-mob/493118/.

THE MACAT LIBRARY
BY DISCIPLINE

AFRICANA STUDIES

Chinua Achebe's *An Image of Africa: Racism in Conrad's Heart of Darkness*
W. E. B. Du Bois's *The Souls of Black Folk*
Zora Neale Huston's *Characteristics of Negro Expression*
Martin Luther King Jr's *Why We Can't Wait*
Toni Morrison's *Playing in the Dark: Whiteness in the American Literary Imagination*

ANTHROPOLOGY

Arjun Appadurai's *Modernity at Large: Cultural Dimensions of Globalisation*
Philippe Ariès's *Centuries of Childhood*
Franz Boas's *Race, Language and Culture*
Kim Chan & Renée Mauborgne's *Blue Ocean Strategy*
Jared Diamond's *Guns, Germs & Steel: the Fate of Human Societies*
Jared Diamond's *Collapse: How Societies Choose to Fail or Survive*
E. E. Evans-Pritchard's *Witchcraft, Oracles and Magic Among the Azande*
James Ferguson's *The Anti-Politics Machine*
Clifford Geertz's *The Interpretation of Cultures*
David Graeber's *Debt: the First 5000 Years*
Karen Ho's *Liquidated: An Ethnography of Wall Street*
Geert Hofstede's *Culture's Consequences: Comparing Values, Behaviors, Institutes and Organizations across Nations*
Claude Lévi-Strauss's *Structural Anthropology*
Jay Macleod's *Ain't No Makin' It: Aspirations and Attainment in a Low-Income Neighborhood*
Saba Mahmood's *The Politics of Piety: The Islamic Revival and the Feminist Subjec*t
Marcel Mauss's *The Gift*

BUSINESS

Jean Lave & Etienne Wenger's *Situated Learning*
Theodore Levitt's *Marketing Myopia*
Burton G. Malkiel's *A Random Walk Down Wall Street*
Douglas McGregor's *The Human Side of Enterprise*
Michael Porter's *Competitive Strategy: Creating and Sustaining Superior Performance*
John Kotter's *Leading Change*
C. K. Prahalad & Gary Hamel's *The Core Competence of the Corporation*

CRIMINOLOGY

Michelle Alexander's *The New Jim Crow: Mass Incarceration in the Age of Colorblindness*
Michael R. Gottfredson & Travis Hirschi's *A General Theory of Crime*
Richard Herrnstein & Charles A. Murray's *The Bell Curve: Intelligence and Class Structure in American Life*
Elizabeth Loftus's *Eyewitness Testimony*
Jay Macleod's *Ain't No Makin' It: Aspirations and Attainment in a Low-Income Neighborhood*
Philip Zimbardo's *The Lucifer Effect*

ECONOMICS

Janet Abu-Lughod's *Before European Hegemony*
Ha-Joon Chang's *Kicking Away the Ladder*
David Brion Davis's *The Problem of Slavery in the Age of Revolution*
Milton Friedman's *The Role of Monetary Policy*
Milton Friedman's *Capitalism and Freedom*
David Graeber's *Debt: the First 5000 Years*
Friedrich Hayek's *The Road to Serfdom*
Karen Ho's *Liquidated: An Ethnography of Wall Street*

The Macat Library By Discipline

John Maynard Keynes's *The General Theory of Employment, Interest and Money*
Charles P. Kindleberger's *Manias, Panics and Crashes*
Robert Lucas's *Why Doesn't Capital Flow from Rich to Poor Countries?*
Burton G. Malkiel's *A Random Walk Down Wall Street*
Thomas Robert Malthus's *An Essay on the Principle of Population*
Karl Marx's *Capital*
Thomas Piketty's *Capital in the Twenty-First Century*
Amartya Sen's *Development as Freedom*
Adam Smith's *The Wealth of Nations*
Nassim Nicholas Taleb's *The Black Swan: The Impact of the Highly Improbable*
Amos Tversky's & Daniel Kahneman's *Judgment under Uncertainty: Heuristics and Biases*
Mahbub Ul Haq's *Reflections on Human Development*
Max Weber's *The Protestant Ethic and the Spirit of Capitalism*

FEMINISM AND GENDER STUDIES

Judith Butler's *Gender Trouble*
Simone De Beauvoir's *The Second Sex*
Michel Foucault's *History of Sexuality*
Betty Friedan's *The Feminine Mystique*
Saba Mahmood's *The Politics of Piety: The Islamic Revival and the Feminist Subject*
Joan Wallach Scott's *Gender and the Politics of History*
Mary Wollstonecraft's *A Vindication of the Rights of Woman*
Virginia Woolf's *A Room of One's Own*

GEOGRAPHY

The Brundtland Report's *Our Common Future*
Rachel Carson's *Silent Spring*
Charles Darwin's *On the Origin of Species*
James Ferguson's *The Anti-Politics Machine*
Jane Jacobs's *The Death and Life of Great American Cities*
James Lovelock's *Gaia: A New Look at Life on Earth*
Amartya Sen's *Development as Freedom*
Mathis Wackernagel & William Rees's *Our Ecological Footprint*

HISTORY

Janet Abu-Lughod's *Before European Hegemony*
Benedict Anderson's *Imagined Communities*
Bernard Bailyn's *The Ideological Origins of the American Revolution*
Hanna Batatu's *The Old Social Classes And The Revolutionary Movements Of Iraq*
Christopher Browning's *Ordinary Men: Reserve Police Batallion 101 and the Final Solution in Poland*
Edmund Burke's *Reflections on the Revolution in France*
William Cronon's *Nature's Metropolis: Chicago And The Great West*
Alfred W. Crosby's *The Columbian Exchange*
Hamid Dabashi's *Iran: A People Interrupted*
David Brion Davis's *The Problem of Slavery in the Age of Revolution*
Nathalie Zemon Davis's *The Return of Martin Guerre*
Jared Diamond's *Guns, Germs & Steel: the Fate of Human Societies*
Frank Dikotter's *Mao's Great Famine*
John W Dower's *War Without Mercy: Race And Power In The Pacific War*
W. E. B. Du Bois's *The Souls of Black Folk*
Richard J. Evans's *In Defence of History*
Lucien Febvre's *The Problem of Unbelief in the 16th Century*
Sheila Fitzpatrick's *Everyday Stalinism*

Eric Foner's *Reconstruction: America's Unfinished Revolution, 1863-1877*
Michel Foucault's *Discipline and Punish*
Michel Foucault's *History of Sexuality*
Francis Fukuyama's *The End of History and the Last Man*
John Lewis Gaddis's *We Now Know: Rethinking Cold War History*
Ernest Gellner's *Nations and Nationalism*
Eugene Genovese's *Roll, Jordan, Roll: The World the Slaves Made*
Carlo Ginzburg's *The Night Battles*
Daniel Goldhagen's *Hitler's Willing Executioners*
Jack Goldstone's *Revolution and Rebellion in the Early Modern World*
Antonio Gramsci's *The Prison Notebooks*
Alexander Hamilton, John Jay & James Madison's *The Federalist Papers*
Christopher Hill's *The World Turned Upside Down*
Carole Hillenbrand's *The Crusades: Islamic Perspectives*
Thomas Hobbes's *Leviathan*
Eric Hobsbawm's *The Age Of Revolution*
John A. Hobson's *Imperialism: A Study*
Albert Hourani's *History of the Arab Peoples*
Samuel P. Huntington's *The Clash of Civilizations and the Remaking of World Order*
C. L. R. James's *The Black Jacobins*
Tony Judt's *Postwar: A History of Europe Since 1945*
Ernst Kantorowicz's *The King's Two Bodies: A Study in Medieval Political Theology*
Paul Kennedy's *The Rise and Fall of the Great Powers*
Ian Kershaw's *The "Hitler Myth": Image and Reality in the Third Reich*
John Maynard Keynes's *The General Theory of Employment, Interest and Money*
Charles P. Kindleberger's *Manias, Panics and Crashes*
Martin Luther King Jr's *Why We Can't Wait*
Henry Kissinger's *World Order: Reflections on the Character of Nations and the Course of History*
Thomas Kuhn's *The Structure of Scientific Revolutions*
Georges Lefebvre's *The Coming of the French Revolution*
John Locke's *Two Treatises of Government*
Niccolò Machiavelli's *The Prince*
Thomas Robert Malthus's *An Essay on the Principle of Population*
Mahmood Mamdani's *Citizen and Subject: Contemporary Africa And The Legacy Of Late Colonialism*
Karl Marx's *Capital*
Stanley Milgram's *Obedience to Authority*
John Stuart Mill's *On Liberty*
Thomas Paine's *Common Sense*
Thomas Paine's *Rights of Man*
Geoffrey Parker's *Global Crisis: War, Climate Change and Catastrophe in the Seventeenth Century*
Jonathan Riley-Smith's *The First Crusade and the Idea of Crusading*
Jean-Jacques Rousseau's *The Social Contract*
Joan Wallach Scott's *Gender and the Politics of History*
Theda Skocpol's *States and Social Revolutions*
Adam Smith's *The Wealth of Nations*
Timothy Snyder's *Bloodlands: Europe Between Hitler and Stalin*
Sun Tzu's *The Art of War*
Keith Thomas's *Religion and the Decline of Magic*
Thucydides's *The History of the Peloponnesian War*
Frederick Jackson Turner's *The Significance of the Frontier in American History*
Odd Arne Westad's *The Global Cold War: Third World Interventions And The Making Of Our Times*

The Macat Library By Discipline

LITERATURE

Chinua Achebe's *An Image of Africa: Racism in Conrad's Heart of Darkness*
Roland Barthes's *Mythologies*
Homi K. Bhabha's *The Location of Culture*
Judith Butler's *Gender Trouble*
Simone De Beauvoir's *The Second Sex*
Ferdinand De Saussure's *Course in General Linguistics*
T. S. Eliot's *The Sacred Wood: Essays on Poetry and Criticism*
Zora Neale Huston's *Characteristics of Negro Expression*
Toni Morrison's *Playing in the Dark: Whiteness in the American Literary Imagination*
Edward Said's *Orientalism*
Gayatri Chakravorty Spivak's *Can the Subaltern Speak?*
Mary Wollstonecraft's *A Vindication of the Rights of Women*
Virginia Woolf's *A Room of One's Own*

PHILOSOPHY

Elizabeth Anscombe's *Modern Moral Philosophy*
Hannah Arendt's *The Human Condition*
Aristotle's *Metaphysics*
Aristotle's *Nicomachean Ethics*
Edmund Gettier's *Is Justified True Belief Knowledge?*
Georg Wilhelm Friedrich Hegel's *Phenomenology of Spirit*
David Hume's *Dialogues Concerning Natural Religion*
David Hume's *The Enquiry for Human Understanding*
Immanuel Kant's *Religion within the Boundaries of Mere Reason*
Immanuel Kant's *Critique of Pure Reason*
Søren Kierkegaard's *The Sickness Unto Death*
Søren Kierkegaard's *Fear and Trembling*
C. S. Lewis's *The Abolition of Man*
Alasdair MacIntyre's *After Virtue*
Marcus Aurelius's *Meditations*
Friedrich Nietzsche's *On the Genealogy of Morality*
Friedrich Nietzsche's *Beyond Good and Evil*
Plato's *Republic*
Plato's *Symposium*
Jean-Jacques Rousseau's *The Social Contract*
Gilbert Ryle's *The Concept of Mind*
Baruch Spinoza's *Ethics*
Sun Tzu's *The Art of War*
Ludwig Wittgenstein's *Philosophical Investigations*

POLITICS

Benedict Anderson's *Imagined Communities*
Aristotle's *Politics*
Bernard Bailyn's *The Ideological Origins of the American Revolution*
Edmund Burke's *Reflections on the Revolution in France*
John C. Calhoun's *A Disquisition on Government*
Ha-Joon Chang's *Kicking Away the Ladder*
Hamid Dabashi's *Iran: A People Interrupted*
Hamid Dabashi's *Theology of Discontent: The Ideological Foundation of the Islamic Revolution in Iran*
Robert Dahl's *Democracy and its Critics*
Robert Dahl's *Who Governs?*
David Brion Davis's *The Problem of Slavery in the Age of Revolution*

Alexis De Tocqueville's *Democracy in America*
James Ferguson's *The Anti-Politics Machine*
Frank Dikotter's *Mao's Great Famine*
Sheila Fitzpatrick's *Everyday Stalinism*
Eric Foner's *Reconstruction: America's Unfinished Revolution, 1863-1877*
Milton Friedman's *Capitalism and Freedom*
Francis Fukuyama's *The End of History and the Last Man*
John Lewis Gaddis's *We Now Know: Rethinking Cold War History*
Ernest Gellner's *Nations and Nationalism*
David Graeber's *Debt: the First 5000 Years*
Antonio Gramsci's *The Prison Notebooks*
Alexander Hamilton, John Jay & James Madison's *The Federalist Papers*
Friedrich Hayek's *The Road to Serfdom*
Christopher Hill's *The World Turned Upside Down*
Thomas Hobbes's *Leviathan*
John A. Hobson's *Imperialism: A Study*
Samuel P. Huntington's *The Clash of Civilizations and the Remaking of World Order*
Tony Judt's *Postwar: A History of Europe Since 1945*
David C. Kang's *China Rising: Peace, Power and Order in East Asia*
Paul Kennedy's *The Rise and Fall of Great Powers*
Robert Keohane's *After Hegemony*
Martin Luther King Jr.'s *Why We Can't Wait*
Henry Kissinger's *World Order: Reflections on the Character of Nations and the Course of History*
John Locke's *Two Treatises of Government*
Niccolò Machiavelli's *The Prince*
Thomas Robert Malthus's *An Essay on the Principle of Population*
Mahmood Mamdani's *Citizen and Subject: Contemporary Africa And The Legacy Of
Late Colonialism*
Karl Marx's *Capital*
John Stuart Mill's *On Liberty*
John Stuart Mill's *Utilitarianism*
Hans Morgenthau's *Politics Among Nations*
Thomas Paine's *Common Sense*
Thomas Paine's *Rights of Man*
Thomas Piketty's *Capital in the Twenty-First Century*
Robert D. Putman's *Bowling Alone*
John Rawls's *Theory of Justice*
Jean-Jacques Rousseau's *The Social Contract*
Theda Skocpol's *States and Social Revolutions*
Adam Smith's *The Wealth of Nations*
Sun Tzu's *The Art of War*
Henry David Thoreau's *Civil Disobedience*
Thucydides's *The History of the Peloponnesian War*
Kenneth Waltz's *Theory of International Politics*
Max Weber's *Politics as a Vocation*
Odd Arne Westad's *The Global Cold War: Third World Interventions And The Making Of Our Times*

POSTCOLONIAL STUDIES

Roland Barthes's *Mythologies*
Frantz Fanon's *Black Skin, White Masks*
Homi K. Bhabha's *The Location of Culture*
Gustavo Gutiérrez's *A Theology of Liberation*
Edward Said's *Orientalism*
Gayatri Chakravorty Spivak's *Can the Subaltern Speak?*

The Macat Library By Discipline

PSYCHOLOGY

Gordon Allport's *The Nature of Prejudice*
Alan Baddeley & Graham Hitch's *Aggression: A Social Learning Analysis*
Albert Bandura's *Aggression: A Social Learning Analysis*
Leon Festinger's *A Theory of Cognitive Dissonance*
Sigmund Freud's *The Interpretation of Dreams*
Betty Friedan's *The Feminine Mystique*
Michael R. Gottfredson & Travis Hirschi's *A General Theory of Crime*
Eric Hoffer's *The True Believer: Thoughts on the Nature of Mass Movements*
William James's *Principles of Psychology*
Elizabeth Loftus's *Eyewitness Testimony*
A. H. Maslow's *A Theory of Human Motivation*
Stanley Milgram's *Obedience to Authority*
Steven Pinker's *The Better Angels of Our Nature*
Oliver Sacks's *The Man Who Mistook His Wife For a Hat*
Richard Thaler & Cass Sunstein's *Nudge: Improving Decisions About Health, Wealth and Happiness*
Amos Tversky's *Judgment under Uncertainty: Heuristics and Biases*
Philip Zimbardo's *The Lucifer Effect*

SCIENCE

Rachel Carson's *Silent Spring*
William Cronon's *Nature's Metropolis: Chicago And The Great West*
Alfred W. Crosby's *The Columbian Exchange*
Charles Darwin's *On the Origin of Species*
Richard Dawkin's *The Selfish Gene*
Thomas Kuhn's *The Structure of Scientific Revolutions*
Geoffrey Parker's *Global Crisis: War, Climate Change and Catastrophe in the Seventeenth Century*
Mathis Wackernagel & William Rees's *Our Ecological Footprint*

SOCIOLOGY

Michelle Alexander's *The New Jim Crow: Mass Incarceration in the Age of Colorblindness*
Gordon Allport's *The Nature of Prejudice*
Albert Bandura's *Aggression: A Social Learning Analysis*
Hanna Batatu's *The Old Social Classes And The Revolutionary Movements Of Iraq*
Ha-Joon Chang's *Kicking Away the Ladder*
W. E. B. Du Bois's *The Souls of Black Folk*
Émile Durkheim's *On Suicide*
Frantz Fanon's *Black Skin, White Masks*
Frantz Fanon's *The Wretched of the Earth*
Eric Foner's *Reconstruction: America's Unfinished Revolution, 1863-1877*
Eugene Genovese's *Roll, Jordan, Roll: The World the Slaves Made*
Jack Goldstone's *Revolution and Rebellion in the Early Modern World*
Antonio Gramsci's *The Prison Notebooks*
Richard Herrnstein & Charles A Murray's *The Bell Curve: Intelligence and Class Structure in American Life*
Eric Hoffer's *The True Believer: Thoughts on the Nature of Mass Movements*
Jane Jacobs's *The Death and Life of Great American Cities*
Robert Lucas's *Why Doesn't Capital Flow from Rich to Poor Countries?*
Jay Macleod's *Ain't No Makin' It: Aspirations and Attainment in a Low Income Neighborhood*
Elaine May's *Homeward Bound: American Families in the Cold War Era*
Douglas McGregor's *The Human Side of Enterprise*
C. Wright Mills's *The Sociological Imagination*

Thomas Piketty's *Capital in the Twenty-First Century*
Robert D. Putman's *Bowling Alone*
David Riesman's *The Lonely Crowd: A Study of the Changing American Character*
Edward Said's *Orientalism*
Joan Wallach Scott's *Gender and the Politics of History*
Theda Skocpol's *States and Social Revolutions*
Max Weber's *The Protestant Ethic and the Spirit of Capitalism*

THEOLOGY

Augustine's *Confessions*
Benedict's *Rule of St Benedict*
Gustavo Gutiérrez's *A Theology of Liberation*
Carole Hillenbrand's *The Crusades: Islamic Perspectives*
David Hume's *Dialogues Concerning Natural Religion*
Immanuel Kant's *Religion within the Boundaries of Mere Reason*
Ernst Kantorowicz's *The King's Two Bodies: A Study in Medieval Political Theology*
Søren Kierkegaard's *The Sickness Unto Death*
C. S. Lewis's *The Abolition of Man*
Saba Mahmood's *The Politics of Piety: The Islamic Revival and the Feminist Subject*
Baruch Spinoza's *Ethics*
Keith Thomas's *Religion and the Decline of Magic*

Printed in the United States
by Baker & Taylor Publisher Services